Cover illustration by
Chris Gray

Published by

Douglas Barry Publications

Kemp House
152 - 160 City Road
London
EC1V 2NX
ENGLAND

Tel 0870 879 3828
Fax 0870 879 2865
E-mail info@DouglasBarry.com
Web www.douglasbarry.com

FIRST PUBLISHED IN THE U.K. 2010

My Soul Purpose

British Library - A CIP Catalogue
record for this book is available
from the British Library.

I.S.B.N.   978-0-9553122-7-4

This book is dedicated to my three wonderful children,
Neil, Gareth and Victoria. Thank you all. I love you.

Content

Who I am?   p. 17

How did I get here?   p. 25

What do I do?   p. 37

My beliefs   p. 41

My first public demonstration   p. 45

How does it work – technique   p. 47

Becoming a Medium   p. 51

Preparation   p. 57

What are Chakras/Psychic Centres?   p. 59

The Aura   p. 63

Psychic, Clairvoyant, Medium?   p. 67

Recognising your potential   p. 71

Opening up and Closing Down to Spirit   p. 75

Linking to spirit   p. 77

Interpreting or Translating information   p. 91

Psychometry   p. 95

Children - is it an imaginary friend?   p. 99

Healing   p.103

Astral Travel   p.108

Spirit Guides and Helpers   p.109

Psychic Self Defence   p.111

Death – what is it we fear?   p.115

Measure of success   p.119

Remember   p.121

Conclusion   p.125

Forward

*"If you can't explain it simply, you don't understand it well enough"...
Albert Einstein*

I would also like to thank the many people who have helped me to get where I am today with my spiritual growth, beliefs and development.

I have had some amazing teachers at some remarkable centres, The Arthur Findlay College being one.

We should also realise that every one we meet, no matter if we know them or not, teach us something. We should learn to recognize this.

My children who have been my most amazing inspiration in that they have had to put up with me and my beliefs and the very many people/strangers visiting our house, and my constant searching. They have always been so supportive of who I am and what I do. Bit of a quirky, eccentric Mum at times, but have always loved you all.

All my friends, who again have been so supportive and have given me the "kick" that I have needed from time to time, in fact many times.

And most importantly of all, my Spirit friends, including all my relatives that have passed, without whom I would not be doing this work at all and would not be able to work on a daily basis helping people from all walks of life – how lucky am I.

All the wonderful people who come to see me for readings and teaching.

My dear friend Mary Edwards, who was very supportive of my work and who set up the Mary Edwards Spiritual Chapel in Ewell Village, and who passed to spirit in May 2008.

Bill Landis, who I had the privilege of working with. He was a great "old school" medium, and passed to spirit in June 2009.

There are many books on the subject of mediumship development, some of which are easier to read than others, but my aim is to try and make this a very simple process of understanding. I was actually asked to write this book as I speak, so here we go. Good luck and enjoy the experiences.

How do I explain what I do. I talk to dead people! It is very difficult sometimes to explain what I actually do. In fact when it came to writing this book, I realised that over the years I actually do not prepare any of my teaching material, that when I start to teach, spirit "take over" and they do it all for me and with me.

So at this point of the book I am asking spirit to help to explain who I am, why I'm doing what I do and how the teaching, for me anyway, works.

Who am I?

"I am afraid to show you who I really am, because if I show you who I really am, you might not like it – and that's all I got"...Sabrina Ward Harrison

I am just an ordinary person, with an ability to link to the spirit world. When I first started this spiritual pathway I never imagined in a million years that I would be doing such an amazing job and helping and touching people every day, across the world. My reason for going to a spiritual church initially was to get help for myself. I thank the spirit world for persisting with me and working with me constantly and giving me this opportunity. My soul purpose now is to help as many people as I can to understand and believe in the spirit world, we are not alone, we have unseen helpers with us at all times. Trust that they are there and believe they can help.

I was born in Billericay, Essex in February 1955. I am the eldest of 6 children, and have 1 brother and 4 sisters. My Mum, Val Day (nee Sarfas) and all her family are from London/Essex, and my Dad, Edward Day, is from Cardiff. I was 18 months old when the family moved from Essex to Cardiff.

Wales is an incredible country. What is very special about Wales though, is the uniqueness of the culture and the people. Their love of Music, Rugby, Mining, sense of family and community, competition (Eisteddfords) etc. The coming together. The majority of people in Wales are connected to at least one of these things in their lifetime. In schools in Wales the emphasis on music and competition is very important, well it was in the schools that I was fortunate to attend.

My family were all very musical. My Grandad on Dad's side was a violin and clarinet player in a military band and had been schooled in India in a military school. My Dad, had the most amazing voice – we always said he sang like Frank Sinatra. When he was in the army, he used to entertain the

17

troops by singing on the ships when he was going back and forward to Korea. His brothers and sisters all either sang or played musical instruments or both. My Mums family were all musical also, playing various instruments and singing.

I realised quite late on in my life that at a very young age, this very shy young person was able to achieve all of these public performances but I felt as if I was hiding behind and being protected by the voice, the violin, the orchestra, the piano and I never believed it was actually me up there doing it. I suppose I would just get totally lost in what I was doing.

Recently I became aware that I was still doing the same thing now working with Spirit. A friend of mine who came to a theatre performance said that he could not believe that I was so nervous and insecure before and after a performance, when during the actual event I was so confident. I said to him that's because it's not me doing it, its them!!! Again being lost to it, totally submerged in it.

Even though I was shy, I was quite a strong character in lots of ways and if I wanted to do something I usually did and succeeded at it.

Because of his upbringing, my Dad used to get my brother and sisters performing at Christmas family parties. Boxing Day was traditionally the day when all the families got together and everyone had to get up and do their party piece. Well he trained us for weeks before and like the like the Von Trapp family from the Sound of Music, us six used to get up and do our turn also.

I sang publicly from the age of 8, being in the school choir (Windor Clive Juniors, Ely), church choir (Church of the Resurrection, Ely), local choir (Ely Girls Choir), and brownies (Congregational Church, Ely) where I also sang at their once a month special services.

The Ely Girls Choir had a fabulous choir master, Ieuan Lewis, and a fantastic reputation. Mr Lewis was actually one of the teachers at Windsor Clive

Junior School. He was fascinated by the Vienna Boys Choir and had wanted to set up a similar boys choir, but could not get enough boys interested in our area at the time. So he set up the girls choir instead. He was such a perfectionist and the choir was amazing. We had the opportunity of entering our choir at Llangollen for the international Eisteddford. There were 36 choirs from across the world in that competition. We were the youngest group and we came 6th. A great achievement and he was so proud and we were all so excited by this.

When we were at Llangollen we stayed in a school hall and had to sleep on camp beds. In the night time the youngest of us had to go to bed when the older girls were allowed to stay up. I was only about 10 at this time and remember one night not wanting to go to sleep so we decided to entertain ourselves. We all had to do a "party piece". I decided to impersonate Harry Secombe, and stuffed a pillow up my nightie, stood on the camp bed and was singing to my heart's content, when in came Mr Lewis, obviously wondering what we were all up to, and as he did the bed ripped and I went hurtling to the ground.

I remember when I was 10 and only had a year to go at junior school, the school introduced violins and other instruments. I wanted to learn to play one of these but was told that as I only had a year left at the school they would not let me. They wanted to give this opportunity to children with 2 years remaining at the school.

Well, I was not happy with this and got my Mum on the case. And hey presto, I was told that I was able to learn. I made a pact with myself that I would always, for as long as I could, come back and support the school orchestra, which I did until I was 19, when I moved to Germany to live. I went on to be able to play the violin for the Cardiff Junior and Senior orchestras reaching first desk position which was quite scary as you are right in the front line.

I also played various other instruments including guitar, piano, banjo (a little), recorder, glockenspiel.

There were various other things that got me up in front of people during my early life. I mentioned earlier Eisteddfords in Wales. Each school used to have this competition for St. David's Day, 1st March, and we would again play instruments, narrate Welsh poems, sing accompanied and unaccompanied.

I was able to speak Welsh at this time and once a week we would have a welsh assembly at school and I would always be picked to read the bible in Welsh. The orchestra used to play at our school assemblies, and I was always jumping around, between singing, playing, reading. Was quite funny thinking back on it now.

From a very young age I had this wierd fascination for graveyards. I never knew where this came from, but would spend hours in them when I got the chance.

I was one of these children who, I thought, was not brilliant at anything in particular, just average BUT always had a go at as many things as I could, especially if it was to do with music.

We lived in a part of Cardiff that was not the best and we came from a humble background, never a lot of money, which was always made more difficult due to the fact that there were so many of us in the family. But we were always out doing things. I remember my Mum and Dad used to take us out walking to so many wonderful places and we would go miles, and never complain – well not that I can remember anyway. We would pack our own picnics so that when we went out we didn't have to spend a lot of money. It was always such fun. We were also lucky in that where we lived, on the Grand Avenue, there were huge oval greens all the way up the centre of the road and the green in front of our house was our playing field and there were always lots of kids around to play with.

I remember always being made fun of at school because of our surname, which up until I was 13 was Cockaday. You can imagine the things they said. Then after having the name changed by Deed Poll to Day, even more fun and ridicule. It never stopped.

I went from Windsor Clive Junior School to Glan Ely High School and was there for 2 years only. During this time again I did as much as I could with music and singing. Moving up the ranks in the orchestras I belonged to. At this school I always did well academically, no Einstein, but I was in the top 3, so not too bad.

I remember an instance here where one of the boys in my class, Stephen, got called out of the class one day. He was told that his father had been killed in a lorry accident. I was really moved by this. I think it hit home as my Dad was a lorry driver also. For Stephen it was obviously a very difficult time and when he eventually came back to school I would try and help him, talk to him as much as I could. The others in the class were not so nice about it, as kids are I guess. Without realising what I was doing I was using my natural healing abilities.

I also had a friend, Mary at that time who came from a difficult background. She was from a single parent family, which was not so common in those days. I never asked why, because I didn't think it was any of our business, but people were always making fun of her and calling her names. I would try to come between her and them and we became good friends. I could never understand why children were so cruel and why they didn't understand that we all had different backgrounds and didn't all have money to buy nice things, or a good home life.

Many times when I was growing up, it was like I would step back from a situation and look at it from the outside, and not realising what I was doing and why. Now of course I do know that I was realising then how different I was and how differently I looked at things. But didn't want to shout about it because I was too shy, didn't have a voice and who would listen to me anyway. But I always tried to help where and when I could.

At the age of 13 there was a special scheme in Cardiff schools which was only used for 2 years where they selected the top students from each school and put them in to one school, and Cardiff High School for Girls was where I ended up. I was one of about 6 girls and about the same boys, who were chosen. I was very excited about this and so were the family, but it put a lot of financial pressure on my parents. The uniform was very expensive and so was the bus journey to school, but I know they were all so proud of the fact that I had been selected.

I used to get up before 6.30am and get breakfast for my brother and sisters. They hated the fact that I was always so chirpy in the mornings. They accused me of being bossy. I was the eldest so felt responsible and used to look after them quite a bit. I always found it easy to take control and be in charge.

My days at Cardiff High School were very difficult. The school was a long way away from home and I found the pressure of being with such clever kids hard. They all came from fairly well to do, professional backgrounds as well, so even more pressure. It always appeared that they were looking down their noses at me. I was lucky though as a girl who had transferred with me, Sharon Haines, became my best friend. She helped me a great deal, I don't know what I would have done without her strength and support.

I was put in the top class but did not do too well in my end of term exams, which really knocked my confidence. After doing so well at the previous school this was a huge blow. I was asked by my form teacher if I wanted to go down a set. My reply to her was "I would rather be bottom of the top set than bottom of the bottom set". I can't believe I was strong enough to say that to her. That's how fierce the competition was. Nevertheless I fought and struggled. One of the saddest things was that I had to give up music as a subject. I did however, keep up the orchestra.

I used to talk to some of the girls about my spiritual experiences and they were fascinated. I remember one day doing a Ouija board in the downstairs cloakroom. It was amazing. I think it was around the time of Donald Campbell's death and guess who came through. Well you can imagine, when the glass was spinning around, the girls all freaked out and ran screaming in all directions. Having done Ouija boards many times since I realise that perhaps my energies were strong then and this was not just a prank with someone "pushing" the glass.

I was only at school until I was 16, in this time I suffered various illnesses that were stress related. A mystery illness that made my legs not work and Alopecia! Very scary. Basically I wasn't coping with the pressure and stress very well.

It was when I was 16 that my Grandad died. My Dad suggested that we do a Ouija board. He had done this many times with his Mum when she was alive. So we all sat down in the back room of our house, where my Grandad had lived. I think there were 6 or 7 of us. We set up the table with the glass and the letters, put candles on and turned out the lights. We started asking the questions and the glass started to move. It was my Nan who was talking to us; she spelt out her name. We then decided that so we knew we were not cheating, that we should ask the questions one at a time, but in our heads, so no one knew what we were asking. The glass kept moving and giving us the answers and we each in turn verified the question we had posed. As my Grandad had only just passed, my question when it came to my turn was "is Grandad with you". The glass spun out of control and then hurtled off the table and smashed. Well you can imagine, again the screams and the scattering of bodies everywhere. Funny now when I think back.

I had great ambitions when I was young, I loved languages so wanted to travel and be a linguist, or a music teacher. But I only stayed on at school until I did my 'O' levels; at which I did really badly. The day I collected my results I felt so humiliated, all the girls going in and getting their results and having done so well. "oh here's Valerie, let's see how you did". That was such a painful day. I didn't want to face any more of that so I left school and went on to Secretarial College, which was so much more relaxed. I did a year there, loved it and did very well.

I started work in an insurance company, which was OK to start with but I realised that if I had to stay in an office like this for the rest of my life that would be awful, I wanted more. So I temped as a junior secretary for over a year, working in many different types of offices. I was still a very shy person and I remember coming home one day saying to my Mum that nobody talked to me. So she said 'well did you talk to them!!!'. So off I went and tried again.

How did I get here?

"On a long journey of human life, faith is the best of companions; it is the best refreshment on the journey: and it is the greatest property"...
Buddha

I was 8 years old when I was first consciously aware of being able to talk to "dead people" although I didn't at the time realise that they were "dead". My Nan on my Dad's side, Hilda, passed to spirit when I was this age. My parents decided that we should move in to her old house to look after my Grandad, William, who was aged about 76 at that time.

I did not want to tell people about my seeing "dead people" as I thought they would think I was mad – if an 8 year old can think that way. So I dealt with these things in my own way. My Mum used to think it was funny though, that from time to time I would mention people in conversations who we had not seen for ages and they would suddenly just turn up on the doorstep or we would hear from them out of the blue. This happened quite a lot.

I was aware of Nan being around me. I suppose the most significant "sightings" was when for instance I was 12 years old. As I've mentioned I was the eldest of 6 children. We lived in a 3 bedroom house, which was quite a squeeze so all us girls had to share a room. My brother had his own room. One night we girls were all fast asleep and something woke me. I opened my eyes and there standing at the end of my bed was my Nan. She was actually standing over one of my sisters, tucking her up in her bed. This particular sister was ill at the time. She just smiled at me and then faded away. This really spooked me but I didn't mention it to anyone at the time. I know now that she was there giving my sister healing, but of course at that time I didn't have a clue why she was there and of course I knew her to be "dead". So this was quite a scary experience for me.

It was quite funny, because after that, I had a nightly ritual before getting into bed. I would tuck the curtain on to the window ledge and line up my dolls on top of this. Then I would check the wardrobe and lock it, check under the bed, then get in to bed, bury my head and not move till morning. The dolls on the window ledge were there just in case anyone came in the window, the wardrobe was to stop anything coming out of there and under the bed, well you never knew!! So this was my regular nightly ritual. Again I don't think I ever explained to my family why I did this. They probably thought, as they still do, that I am little strange.

Then when I was 16, I went into our bathroom and closed the door behind me. Directly in front of you when you walked in was a mirror. This particular day, there in the mirror was my Nan! I turned to check this out behind me in case there was something there or on the door that would reflect but there was nothing on the back of the door and the door was painted white! But there she was in the mirror. This scared me. I was alone in the house but I remember very ceremoniously going to the centre of the house and saying "I know you are there, but I don't understand what's going on and I am afraid, so please go away"… and she did.

There were always strange things going on in our house, things falling off shelves that should never have fallen. People brushing past us on the stairs, but nobody being there; these would always be warnings of things that were about to happen.

I have myself been going to see mediums from the age of 18. I know I said when I was 16 I had asked them to leave me, but that didn't stop me knowing they were still around me and could help me whenever I needed them.

I met my first husband Tony, in the 70's. He was learning to play guitar and had come from a family with a traditional folk music background. He decided to get me to learn to sing folk. We used to practice in our houses all the time. One day we saw an advert for a competition, South Wales Search for a Star! For some unknown reason I thought we should enter. I just had a "feeling" about it and for some reason and somehow we got to the finals.

We were due to get married and I don't know why I felt the urge to see a medium. I chose to see a lovely old lady called Mrs Bradshaw, who lived off Cathedral Road, in Cardiff. I remember on my first visit to her it was like walking in to an old horror movie. Her home was a big Victorian house, and very dark and dingy with lots of old furniture. She sat in a corner which was quite dark too, which added to the eeriness of the setting. She asked if she could hold an item of mine and then proceeded to tell me so many things about my life, my family, and what I would be doing in the future, all of which was accurate. I was astounded. She was an amazing medium. She also told me I would be travelling over water and that my marriage would not last! Obviously, I did not want to hear that! What I didn't know at that time was that my Nan, Hilda, used to visit her and also my Dad's sisters had been to see her.

Another thing I didn't know until about 2000, was that my Nan was a medium in her own right – she used to read people's tea leaves. According to my Dad she had many spooky things happening round the house. For instance, when her Son, Douglas was away at sea, there was a crashing noise in early hours one morning. My Nan came running down the stairs to see what it was and found 7 white chalky dots on the floor. She touched the last one and said "Douglas is dead". He was actually in a convoy of 7 ships. She heard very soon after that his ship had actually been torpedoed and sunk. My Dad told me recently that the same incident happened in the houses of two other family members at exactly the same time. So it looks like I get some of my abilities from my Nan.

On the occasions when I "saw" my Nan after she had passed, she was always dressed in orange. I have since found out that all my brothers and sisters saw her, and that again she was dressed in orange. (Although they have all seen her, they don't like to admit it or talk about it, even now!). I didn't realise how important colours are in the spirit world until much later. I believe orange is a very spiritual colour signifying strength, motivation and determination.

Tony and I got married. He was an RAF policeman at that time and was posted to Germany. When we were there we formed a folk band with two others and toured many of the Army and RAF bases singing in the services folk clubs. At this time I also had a job as a P.A. on the Airforce base and later at the NAAFI Headquarters. Again more experience of being in front of people performing, but again not realising where this was eventually to take me.

Tony was always very spooked by my spiritual stuff. I remember him telling his friends "my wife's spooky but we don't talk about it".

Tony was stationed in Cornwall when I had my first child, Neil, in 1977. We lived in a very small two bedroom house. I was having difficulties coming to terms with a new baby. Who doesn't!! And Neil wasn't the easiest of babies – bless him. However again I just knew that my lovely Nan was always around me, helping and guiding me. It was funny that I just accepted she was there.

One time when my youngest sister came with her friend to visit she had to sleep downstairs. When I got up in the morning she asked why had I come down in the night and opened the door. She said I stood there looking at her and not speaking and then went back upstairs. Of course I hadn't done this at all. So I asked her to describe what she saw, and she said I had an orange dressing gown on. Which I didn't have! The description she actually gave was my (our) Nan.

On another occasion my brother came to visit and told me that Nan had been sitting on the end of his bed talking to him and saying he would be getting engaged to his then girlfriend. Again he described her and the colour she was dressed in was orange.

My son Gareth was born in 1979, in Cardiff after Tony had come out of the RAF. We were settled back in South Wales at this time and he was now working as a civilian policeman. We moved in to a police house where there were often knocks and "bumps in the night" which I just accepted. I had two small babies and I didn't have the time to think any more about it.

I did visit a spiritual church from time to time during this period. But nothing exciting! When the boys were about 4 and 5 we moved to a house near the seaside, in a place called Ogmore By Sea. It was a strange bungalow that had been added to and extended several times. We had all sorts of funny things happening in this house. We would always lock up at night but sometimes would wake up in the morning to find the front door wide open, and sheep in the hallway (we lived on common grazing land!).

One beautiful sunny evening in July we had my nephew, Christopher staying with us. The boys who were of similar ages wanted to watch the Superman video so we all sat down to watch it. The main room to the house was long and had French windows leading out onto the garden. As we were sitting watching the film, there was a knock on the French windows, but there was no one there. So we ignored it. Then another knock only louder, then the doors started shaking quite violently but still nobody was there. Tony got up so see what was going on and I followed on behind him. The boys were still all sitting on the sofa. As we walked up the room we felt someone push past us and the two doors which lead to our bedroom opened on their own.

Our bedroom was the other side of the house to that of the boys so we kept the light on in the hallway between, just in case one of them got up in the night. One particular night I suddenly became aware of the quilt at the end of the bed having been lifted and little hands, like those of a child, touching my toes. I was quite scared, and my mind racing, but did not want to open my eyes thinking that if the boys had come in to the room, the light would be shining into them, but there was no light. I forced myself to go back to sleep. There must be a logical explanation. Next thing I remember Tony leapt out of bed, screaming. He said exactly the same thing had happened to him. We got up and checked the house and there was no one in the house except us and the boys were fast asleep in their beds.

A few days later I was working in the kitchen when all of a sudden a milk bottle smashed in the sink, all 5 doors off the main room slammed shut and a plant trough in front of the French windows fell over scattering plants and earth everywhere, all at exactly the same moment. These incidents all happened in a very short space of time. I often got the smell of flowery perfume in the house – I hate flowery perfume so it wasn't me!

I mentioned these happenings to the locals in the village pub and they started to tell me all sorts of stories about the ghosts in the area, and that apparently our house had been built on the site of an old Quakers meeting place. The previous owner had spoken of strange goings on in our house,......as far as I was concerned that was it! As Tony was a Catholic I went to the Catholic Church and asked the Priest to come out and bless the house – which they did.

At this time I had not explored my psychic/spiritual abilities so was not fully understanding any of this. I now know differently and what this was all about. Looking back, I realise that this was a very difficult time in our marriage and it was like someone was trying to warn me, tell me something, but I was not listening and did not understand. Tony and I split up shortly afterwards.

When I was between 8 and 16 two of my Dad's sisters and their families moved to Australia. We were supposed to follow but circumstances changed and we didn't go. When I was still with Tony I heard that my cousin, Jacqui, who lived in Australia was ill with Cancer. She was in her 20's and had two small children. We had met a few times up to her moving to Australia. This was the time of "snail mail" so I started to write to her to let her know that I was thinking of her and sending her "healing". The relationship between Jacqui and I over the years has strengthened and we are like sisters. So much so that I always "know" when she is not right. Her Mum and Dad have since passed and they always pop in and let me know when something's up. It can be quite spooky and we always laugh about it. I get frustrated with the time difference though, when I feel something it's not always appropriate to call. So I have to be patient and wait. She is very special to me and always will be. I'm sure we were close in a previous lifetime.

I then met Richard who was originally from the same village, but now lived in London and not long afterwards I was moving lock, stock and barrel up the country to be with him. We were married not long afterwards and my daughter Victoria was born in 1989.

I "knew" when I was pregnant, before the testing, I was told by my Nan AND that it would be a girl. I just "knew"! I also "knew" that she had to be called Victoria. What I didn't know at that time was my Nan, who we all knew as Hilda, was actually called Victoria Hilda. It wasn't until after Victoria was born that my Aunty Lynn, told me that Nan would have been very proud that I had called her Victoria. She told me that she had promised her Mum that she would call her first daughter Victoria, but for some reason changed her mind and her Mum was very disappointed. So my Nan got her wish a little later on down the family line.

While I was pregnant, I was made redundant. It was at this time that I set up my own typing services, EBS, which was hard work but very exciting and enjoyable. I remember one of my very first assignments. I was asked if I would be interested in typing a book for the Actor Herbert Lom. Amazing and such a wonderful man. The business grew slowly and it was hard progressing that and looking after 3 small children. Trying to find a balance was not always easy, but somehow things were laid out in front of me, and it happened and I did it all. Thanks to the help of the spirit world. I always thank them for the good and the bad because if we did not have bad experiences how on earth are we supposed to appreciate the good. Thank you! Thank you! Thank you!

I was now in my mid 30's, things were not going smoothly. I was having serious health problems and having problems with my marriage. I needed some help. Where did I turn? What should I do? I just "knew" that the only place I could find the help I needed was through a Spiritual Church.

I had not long moved from South Wales to South East London, I was still not too sure of the area and had not made many friends. To this day I am still not quite sure why, but I decided to ring the local Council and asked them for details of a local Spiritualist Church. They gave me the details of West Wickham Spiritualist Church which was not too far from me and I arranged to go along and see what it was like. I now know that if Spirit mean to get you to work with or for them, they will no matter what. They were trying to help me and trying to make me more aware of my own spiritual gifts and abilities.

I remember walking in to West Wickham Spiritualist Church for the first time, not knowing anybody and feeling very awkward. This was a very unhappy time for me, I looked and felt a wreck. Despite my appearance everyone was very friendly and started chatting to me. I remember the lovely feeling of peace at the end of that service and knew that it was going to help me. Week after week I would go in to the church feeling so down and unhappy, but would come out of there feeling like I had the strength to fight the world and carry on. I made lots of new friends, it was like a weekly fix, like a drug.

I got many messages through the mediums on platform, from my relatives in spirit that were full of comfort and encouragement for me. Many of these messages were written down and I have kept them to this day. I still look at them from time to time and realise just how much it helped me, knowing that I was not alone and that my family and friends who had passed could still help me in my daily life.

West Wickham was an amazing Church and I have a lot of people there to thank for where I am today and what I am doing. They had, and still do have, regular classes, beginners development circle, advanced platform, discussion groups and a speakers class. I was fascinated by all of this and slowly became part of some of the classes and also started training to be a spiritual healer.

A spiritualist Church is not like other churches, yes you get the prayers and the hymns, a talk by the medium (which is usually inspirational), but the second half of the service is given over to the medium to bring messages to members of the audience from their loved ones in spirit. These messages to me prove that the physical body passes over but the spirit continues. There is life after death.

In my time I have seen some superb mediums, some of whom are no longer with us, but who were very inspirational. I had also seen some not so good, and always vowed when I started this work that I would make sure I did it properly, with love, compassion, sincerity and honesty and will always continue to do that.

One week at a Sunday service, a lovely medium called Ian Taylor, who is still out there working for Spirit, gave me a message from my Nan. She told me, through Ian, that I would be working for Spirit, on a platform doing what he was doing. I do remember saying at the time "oh don't be so stupid". How wrong was I? When I joined the various groups/classes within the Church, I had no intention at all of doing what I am doing today. I just went along because I was intrigued by all of this and wanted to learn more.

Looking back over my life I realise now that it has been a series of events, pointing me in the direction of working with Spirit, who have a very strange way of working to get you working with them, and they WILL by hook or by crook get you working for them and with them.

A group of friends within the Church decided to form a home development circle. We were all very inexperienced and didn't know what we were doing really. So for a number of years not much happened. But I just KNEW that this was the right thing to be doing. I KNEW I should be there and keep attending week after week. At that time I was working full time with my business, I had a young family, and at the end of the working day would be shattered, and usually fall asleep on the sofa. However when it was time for me to go to circle I would be woken up just in time – I believe spirit did this! I "needed" to be there. I also realise that although it appeared that I was not learning anything, spirit were working on my spirit! They were preparing me for what I am doing now. At that time I was not in a strong enough position physically or emotionally to be able to deal with that. So it's a good job I was patient or rather, that they were patient with me.

After a few years, this circle disbanded, people needing to move on. I mentioned in Church that I was looking for a new circle, which you always had to be invited to join. My very dear friend Gwen Jenkins, invited me to become a member of her circle. I knew that her circle was a good one to belong to and that she had several working mediums come out of there. On my first week and I got nothing. Then the next week, bingo! All this information was being given to me – it was amazing. The information I was getting was very personal to some of the other circle members. I was so shocked and had no way of knowing any of this beforehand.

Throughout my time at Gwen's circle I had still been continuing with classes at the church and had now reached the advanced platform level and doing OK. This class was where new developing mediums get up and "practice" on a real live audience. I was not confident in what I was doing, and just went along with it all. It was quite scary though standing in front of people and trying to connect to the spirit world. It's not easy, you question yourself so much at this stage in your development, "am I making this up". I always questioned myself, but never my intentions.

The teacher in this class was a wonderful lady who I will always thank for me being where I am, Geraldine Ford. She is a great teacher and medium and had herself been taught by the great Gordon Higginson. She was always full of encouragement and support and really did push us in the class, and was quite a hard task master. When she knew that one of her "fledglings" were ready to do more she would encourage them to go out with her and share a service. One day after class she said to me "you need some outside practice" at which I gulped!! She then said "I am doing a service at Kingston Spiritualist Church on Wednesday, would you like to come along and do the service with me?" Well I didn't dare say no as she could be quite pushy – in a lovely way of course.

Well there I was at Kingston Spiritualist Church for the Wednesday service, and I can't begin to tell you how terrified I was. I introduced myself to the stewards of the church when I got there and was taken to get a cup of tea. We sat and waited for Geraldine to turn up... and we waited... and waited. She didn't turn up, her car had broken down, and guess what - I was left to do the whole service all on my own. I was horrified.

I know now that spirit have a strange way of working with us to get us to do what they want and they had obviously "engineered" this and from then on I didn't look back. I started getting bookings from other Churches, and so it went on. Whenever I speak to Geraldine I always say thank you.

When I first started going out to work in other Churches, Gwen continued to be a constant source of support. She used to come along with me and acted like my "battery source", sending up her love and energy always. She also used to get her friends around to her home in order that I could "practice" on them, giving them a private sitting. She was wonderful to do this for me and I thank her constantly.

So my work with spirit has progressed from here.

What do I do?

"Nirvana or lasting enlightenment or true spiritual growth can be achieved only through persistent exercise of real love"...M.Scott Peck

I was always taught that the job of a medium was to prove that the spirit lives on and that there is no death. I think I have the best job in the world. To be able to connect to spirit and link people to their relatives and friends who have passed on to the realms of spirit is amazing and I am continually surprised by the information I am given from spirit.

It is such a comforting thing for so many people to be able to know that their relatives are out of pain **and** still around them **and** that they can still link to them and communicate. The reassurance from the messages they get helps to give closure, and comfort. I feel that being able to link to the spirit world and give these messages is a healing process. Grieving people need healing and this is what most mediums do for so many people. I often wonder if the person coming for a private sitting, or who gets a message at a public meeting actually realises that that's what this is all about.

I will always continue to work within the Spiritualist Churches as this is where my beginnings were. Most of these audiences already believe that spirit are there with us continually and in an afterlife, that is one of the reasons they continue to go on a regular basis. However I do love working with theatre audiences. I always make a point of asking these audiences if they have been to a mediumship demonstration before. I am always surprised by the number of them that have not. The main reason for this is, unlike the church audiences, they do not necessarily "believe". They come to a mediumship demonstration for various reasons, some out of curiosity, some just get dragged along by their friends or family. They are often there searching, wanting confirmation of a loved one that has passed on still being with them and it's great to be able to prove to them that the spirit does live on and that we **do not** die.

I know when I do theatres, I am still amazed by the number of people who have never been to a public demonstration of mediumship previously, which I have worked out to be about 80% of the audience. I will also guarantee that returning to a theatre in the same geographical area I will always get a completely different audience of whom again 80% are "first timers". I love this and feel that I am helping to spread the word of spirit, that life is eternal.

When you go to a spiritualist church, the majority of the people there are already believers in life after death. So you are "preaching to the converted" if you like. When you do a mediumship demonstration in a theatre or hall you can touch so many more people who don't really "believe" but really want to know that there is life after death and that is where I really love working.

Some people can be put off from going to a church, which for some signifies hymns, a preacher, prayers etc. – early experiences of churches can put people off. Whereas, everyone can go to a theatre, where the demonstration of mediumship, is just that. The majority of people who come to a theatre event are very surprised by what is said and done and most go away convinced!

Today more and more people are being opened up to the awareness of Spirit or "something else". Mediums have a much higher profile on the TV, with many books and films covering the subject. So more and more, when someone does lose a loved one, they do not feel so apprehensive about going to seek out a medium. Most people know someone that has been for a reading or to a public demonstration or have seen programmes on the TV about it, and of course more recently the internet.

If you are looking for a medium try and get a recommendation. If you are looking at someone on the internet for instance, try and look at testimonials. There are places such as the SAGB (Spiritualists Association of Great Britain) and SNU (Spiritualist National Union) who have lists of mediums throughout the country that they can recommend.

In all industries you get good and bad. Spiritualism is just the same. I have dealt with many sceptical people and to date have always managed to convince them that this is for real and not mind reading or making it up!

I remember a very good friend of mine who was fascinated by what I did. He wanted to have a reading but also wanted to take me out for dinner. I said that I would have to do the reading first as I didn't want him to think I had gleaned the information from him over dinner. So we arranged to do the reading, and then go out to dinner on the same evening. This sceptic was so shocked by the reading. He said it was so accurate and was reduced to tears from the emotion of it. He could not believe that I could describe photographs in great detail and give precise information about his parents and what they did when they were here.

I feel that hearing from a loved one in spirit is a healing process. When I first got involved with the Spiritualist Churches I felt that some people thought it was very morbid "talking to the dead", and I think in years gone by people had the attitude that communicating with dead people was morbid and sinister. I know a lot of modern day mediums who do their work and it certainly is none of that. I made sure that when I started out that I would do this work with a lot of fun and happiness.

Think about it for a moment, when your loved ones were here they had a sense of humour (or not in some cases) and just because they are on the other side that does not mean to say that they lose that sense of humour. When I work I always try to bring that element in to the service or demonstration. It's so important for people to laugh and have fun and not be too serious. Bringing the fun element into this work is not being disrespectful to spirit. They want us to enjoy their communication as well as us wanting to enjoy them being there. This is so important for us all to realise.

I think these days many more people from all walks of life, all religions and cultures are searching for things to help them through difficult times. I think that more people are feeling comforted by the fact that their loved ones are still with them and they can ask them for help and guidance just like they did when they were here. Or just knowing that they are out of their pain and discomfort!

I do many readings for people of all religions and recently did a reading for two Israeli ladies who in turn invited me to their country to do readings for family and friends. I have also worked in Greece, America and Australia. Even with a language difficulty I have managed to convey the message of love and hope.

People just need to recognise that loved ones are listening to them and responding. You just have to learn to recognise the way they do this. It may not be the same way that a medium gets the message but they will get their message through to you somehow. This could be in the form of music that they would have liked, something someone says, something you read, or even a sign on a vehicle!

People are looking more and more to prove that there is more to life than this!!! That is what as a medium, by linking to spirit I am able to do.

My Beliefs

I was brought up strict Church of England and went to church regularly. However as I grew up I did go to other denomination churches. The reason for this was I had the opportunity to sing. This was always one of my great loves, so the more the merrier. Again putting myself in the forefront, performing in front of people. I still find this strange seeing as I was such a shy little girl.

So Sundays were always church days. One Sunday, when I was just 13 years old I came home from church and horrified my Mum by saying that I would not be going back. When she asked why, I explained that "I don't understand the high brow language from the Vicar and I don't believe that we are born, live our lives and learn all we learn just to die and get buried in a box and that's the end of us. There just has to be more to life than that". I believe that this was when I started my spiritual search.

I still do believe in God, but my understanding now is that God is the life force within us all. We are all connected to that infinite energy source, we are all one. This takes away the barriers of religions. We are all interconnected in this world and we can all help one another just by believing and working with that knowledge.

As I have already mentioned, I was aware of spirit from around the age of 8. By the time I was 16 my Grandad was in an old people's hospital. Initially he went in to the hospital to give my Mum some rest, as coping with a senile old person, 6 young children and a full time job was very difficult for her. When he was in the hospital staff could not believe that she had coped for so long with him at home and it was decided he should stay indefinitely. He was a lovely old man, funny and always humming along to the music in his head, playing tricks on us kids and doing daft things like putting pegs on our dolls ears, (or his for that matter) as earrings. Maybe that's where I get my madness from!

Christmas 1972, was a busy time for my Mum, she asked if I could go and visit Grandad and take in his Christmas gifts, which I did on Christmas Eve. He seemed to me the same, but something was nagging inside me and I couldn't work out what it was. I remember coming home from that visit fairly shaken. Mum asked me what was wrong and I said that I didn't think Grandad would be with us for much longer, I didn't know why I knew but I just "knew".

On Christmas Day my sister and I had arranged for our boyfriends to come to visit in the afternoon. It was very strange as all day the door kept knocking, but as the door was partially glazed, we could see that there was actually no-one outside the door. This went on for a few hours. We were all getting a bit frustrated with this continual knocking and wondered if the boys were playing tricks, which was usual for them. So I opened the door, but there was no-one there. Within half an hour of me doing this we had a call from the hospital to say that my Grandad had actually died at roughly the time I had opened the door. We often say that it was almost like he was knocking to come back home.

My Nan and Grandad on my mum's side were Londoners but due to ill health had lived in Wales with my Mum for the last 15 years of their lives. My Nan was blind and Grandad was finding it more and more difficult to cope on his own. At this time I actually lived in London myself. It was coming up to Christmas 1997 and something was nagging at me to go home for a visit. It was good to see everyone and they were all in good health. However 2 weeks later my Grandad died unexpectedly.

My Nan was devastated when he died, and her health started to deteriorate. I went down to Wales to visit her shortly afterwards, as she was now in a nursing home. She was very intrigued by what I did with my spiritual work and she questioned me about my beliefs, how many people "believed" and went to these Spiritual Churches and would she really "see" and "be with" my Grandad again! Of course I did my best to try and convince her that she would be with him again and that he was with her all the time.

How lovely to see that smile on her face when I confirmed to her that that would be the case and they would be together forever – they had been together over 60 years in their earthly life! Two weeks later my Nan died, just six weeks after my Grandad. I think she died of a broken heart as she couldn't bear to be without him. I have since had many "visits" from all my Grandparents. They always seem to come when there is a need, which is extremely comforting to me.

My Grandad who had been a carpenter visited me one day when I had just finished laying laminate flooring throughout the ground floor of my house. I ached from head to foot and was heading up to bed, when I heard him say to me "well done". How proud was I?

They have been with me ever since they passed and have been through in many messages from other mediums as well as communicating directly with me. I also get communication from my relatives for other family members. Not long after my Aunty Dorothy died, I was at home alone and had just got into the shower when I heard a ladies voice, as clear as a bell telling me to "phone Hazel".

Hazel is my cousin, Dorothy's daughter. I thought this was a strange message to get because I knew that Hazel worked full time and as this was mid-morning, was not likely to be at home. However she (my aunt) had sounded very insistent that I call, so I got out of the shower and called Hazel. To my surprise she was actually at home. She was feeling very down, was not well and really missing her mum. So I told her why I was calling and about her mum telling me to phone and was able to tell her that her mum was still there with her and she had wanted her to know that. This helped my cousin a great deal. And she was so grateful that I had passed this message on to her.

Recently I was washing glasses, which I am always careful with as I have a fear of them breaking in the water! I was minding my own business concentrating on washing them carefully and one just shattered in my hand. I mean shattered, broke into little squares. I instantly threw them down and shouted at spirit "I don't like that, what's this all about".

The following day, which was a Saturday, my daughter and I were preparing our pre-Christmas dinner. We were all going to be in different places for Christmas Day, I was going to be in Wales, Gareth in America, Neil in England and Victoria in Australia, so had decided to do it early when we would all be together. Victoria had already realised that she had forgotten her passport when she came home from university and knew that she would have to go back and get it before her trip which was just 3 days later. Both she and I were travelling (me to Israel) on the Tuesday.

So there we are preparing the vegetables and all of a sudden she said "oh that felt like someone walked right passed me". She thought it was one of her brothers, but they were not in the kitchen. So I told her to say hello and thank you for being there! Which she did. The conversation switched for some reason, to her passport and how annoyed she was that she had forgotten it. She mentioned that it ran out in February. I was surprised and said that I thought she needed 6 months left on a passport to be able to travel. She immediately got on the phone to the Passport Office and of course it was the case. However being Saturday all the passport offices were closed. The earliest appointment we could get in London was Tuesday – which was no good as she was travelling that day. So we managed to get an appointment in Newport, Wales for 8am on the Monday morning. I am convinced that this was one of my grandparents who were trying to help us, letting us know that there was a problem. Imagine how devastating it would have been if she had arrived at the airport to be told she could not travel. Thank you, thank you, thank you!!!

It is wonderful to think that all the people that I have known in this earthly life are still there in spirit, and when I need them I know they will always be there to help and guide.

Everybody should have this belief.

My first public demonstration

My first public demonstration was because my wonderful teacher, Geraldine felt I needed some "outside practice". Lacking in confidence as I was, I still needed that extra shove to get myself "out there".

I was still attending the Advanced Platform class at West Wickham Church, Kent. There was another student there who actually was running the Sevenoaks Awareness Centre. His name was David Ingman.

David approached me one night at class and said that he had had a cancellation for the following Sunday and asked if I would like to be the Medium at the service. I was quite taken aback. I said to him "I am not capable, and definitely not ready, why not ask others in the class who were far more experienced than me". He would not take no for an answer insisted that spirit had told him to ask me and asked me to consider the offer. It was agreed that I would think about it overnight and come back to him in the morning. That night I really tossed and turned, not sure what to do.

I went to work in the morning and at 9am I picked up the phone, called David and as quickly as I could, said, "I don't know why I am saying this but yes I will do the service" and then quickly hung up!

The Sunday arrived when I was to do this service and I remember being so nervous. What I had let myself in for and why? I put my trust in the spirit world and did what I had to do. It was an amazing evening. Spirit worked so well with me and the people at Sevenoaks were fantastic. They knew that I was a nervous beginner and treated me so well. This centre has always had a special place in my heart since.

This boosted my confidence no end. Why did I not just TRUST that Spirit would NOT let me down?

So now I had been thrown in the deep end twice and on both occasions spirit did NOT let me down but as a medium one is very sensitive and the feeling of nervousness on each of these sessions is indescribable.

That was the beginning of my public performances but also at that time I had started doing private readings for people. This had been arranged by Gwen Jenkins, my lovely mentor from West Wickham Church. She got me doing private readings on her friends for practice.

I realise now that sometimes things happen in life apparently by accident which are very much meant to "be". Many such things have happened in my life since but I know now that these are not by accident!

Spirit certainly knew me and certainly knew that this was the way they would get me working for them.

I would like to say that in all the time I have been working for and with spirit I have always worked full time which has sometimes been difficult juggling everything. I had built up quite a successful business and in 2002 I had great misfortune of losing everything at the hands of some very unscrupulous ruthless people. I tried very hard to build up the business again, but kept coming up against obstacles and I could not work out why.

Then in 2007 I was still battling with growing business issues, and was preparing to go to Australia to visit family for a special occasion, when again I was let down at the last minute. I had just about had enough at this point and screamed at spirit "OK I am listening and I will work for you solely". I literally did scream.

And that's what I did. I went to Australia, everything went pear shaped when I was away, and I came back to face the music. I then made my decision to give up the business for good. That was the best decision I ever made. I am now working full time with spirit, helping and healing and teaching and so much more. What more could I ask for? What more could I want?

How does it work?
Technique

How do you explain how you communicate with the spirits of the departed or 'talk to dead people'?

My mother was a psychiatric nurse for over 30 years and I remember after I started on this spiritual pathway, having a conversation with her about patients at the hospital. She had often mentioned people who had voices in their heads telling them to do things. Others holding a conversation with nobody. After learning to do what I do I think it very sad that some of those people may have genuinely been seeing and hearing but people around them obviously just did not understand or were frightened so they were locked up in institutions or sent to the "mad house".

I was lucky to be a part of a TV programme called Jane Goldman Investigates, where she was being taught, amongst other things, how to be a medium. In the mediumship programme she actually investigated the psychiatric angle of "talking to the dead" or the dead talking to us.

A good way of describing how it works would be to imagine the feeling of day dreaming, letting your mind wander and just allowing "things" to pop in to your head. We as adults sometimes find this difficult to do as we have too much "stuff" going on in our heads, and our lives are so busy we just don't have the time to just stop and listen. Children on the other hand are great at doing this, they don't even think about it – it is just there for them and they just do it automatically. I wish a lot more parents were aware of this ability within their children.

It is difficult explaining the techniques of communication. I have been seeing things since I was 8 and have just "accepted" that they are there. I am one of the lucky ones I suppose. However I have to teach people all the time and some people just won't "accept", they question themselves, their teacher, and spirit constantly. This is a good thing I know.

Firstly it **is** important to remember that we are **all** born with the ability to communicate with spirit for healing and mediumship purposes. Sadly we get to a certain point in our lives when the big wide world takes over and this ability/skill is often pushed aside. So many children are open to and aware of spirit. I am sure that a lot of you reading this will have heard of children who have imaginary friends. Well this is not necessarily the case, are they imaginary or real? In my own case, my brothers and sisters have all being seeing things from a very early age, but don't like to talk about it now.

People get their first "awareness" for different reasons and at different times in their lives. This could be a trauma, the loss of a loved one, illness or it just could be the right time!

Learning

At this point I would advise that it is always best, as with most subjects, to learn with supervision. This way you will be given the correct guide lines and encouragement. Although there is a lot of information contained in this book about learning to connect to spirit, I would always recommend that learning to be a medium should be done under supervision, and also in a hands on manner.

There are many good teachers and groups out there. I did many classes at the Arthur Findlay College of Psychic Studies, in Essex. They have some amazing teachers and a variety of different courses running throughout the year. There are many learning facilities, some of which are detailed at the end of this book.

Please always remember this:
Please remember, that reading this book, and doing the various exercises, does not make you a medium. It takes years of dedication and training and you may well need the guidance of an experienced teacher/medium who can tell you when you are ready to move forward.

I am fortunate to now be teaching mediumship myself. I have had some amazing teachers over the last 20 years and I love the fact that I now can pass on some of my skills and knowledge and hopefully help to get a new breed of mediums working with spirit and working for humanity. I think this is the ultimate aim, getting as many people to be spiritually aware, not necessarily to get up and work on the platform but to help themselves and others on a daily basis.

I always tell my students that I may not know it all, but what knowledge I have, I will gladly pass on and if I see students getting up there and doing it bigger and better than me, wow, I will be so pleased and so proud.

Many of my friends and relatives who have passed to spirit actually come back in my classes. This is a constant source of amusement to my students who can't get over how many "dead people" I know. Many in the spirit world want to continue to work with us and for us. So even if you don't think you have this ability, remember you were born with it, and with proper training, you can all regain these skills and learn to link to the spirit world again. Later on I will take you through some exercises to be able to give you a taster of how you can practice linking to spirit.

Becoming a Medium

I have always been taught that a medium is there to prove that life is eternal and there is no death and that the spirit lives on. A lot of people who end up as a medium have maybe become curious when they have lost someone close to them. Other people just need the reassurance that they are not alone and that there is something more to life. Then there are those who get to the latter part of their life and realise that they are not immortal and question what happens to us after we die.

As I have explained previously, having been consciously aware of spirit since I was 8 years old, it is difficult to explain. So this is a very difficult question for me to answer as I have been "seeing and hearing" things for such a long time, to me its like – well brushing your teeth! I just have always had them there so there was always a total acceptance and I never questioned it. However I have had to learn to focus my psychic abilities in order to do this work.

I recently spoke to a lady whose husband was dying from Cancer and she wanted to learn how to link so she could still stay in touch with him after his passing.

Most people are actually born with the ability to connect to spirit but they just don't realise it. If more people took the time realise this and learn to focus, there would be a lot more people who were working with spirit, again not necessarily on a public platform but just for themselves.

They need to realise that spirit are with us all, all of the time.

People who are experiencing spirit for the first time can find this very frightening. I always explain to people that there is nothing to be frightened of. Spirits are only there to help us. These spirits are mostly people you would have known when they were alive and who would have loved and cared for you, and just because they have passed to spirit, that is not going to change. They are only wanting to comfort and help us.

On the other hand, there are people in spirit who were not nice to you when they were here. A lot of these realise the error of their ways when they get to spirit, and in many cases my experience shows that these spirits come back to make amends and to try and help in any way that they can. As if they were saying they're "sorry".

Years ago, mediumship used to be a "behind closed doors" thing. Nowadays, with TV, books and internet coverage of mediumship there is an opportunity for everyone who wants to know and learn more. More and more people are becoming interested and intrigued. I find this very heart warming and call this my "ripple on the pond " effect, spreading the word so to speak.

More and more people are realising that they have an ability, are less frightened by it, and want to know "can I do this, how do I do it?" and "where can I learn?"

Firstly we have to train our minds to be able to recognise that spirit can connect with us. We have to recognise what is spirit and what is us, or our minds. Meditation is a way of learning to focus your mind, trying to block out the outside world and then concentrating on what is in our head. It is sometimes difficult to be able to block out the every-day thoughts that are always with us. But don't worry too much about this at this stage. If it is meant to work for you then it will – Trust!

Visualisation is a great way of learning how to focus, enabling you to create something from nothing in your mind. There are many exercises you can do to expand this ability. Here are a few examples:

Exercise 1

Look out of the window. What do you see? Write it down.

Now just sit quietly, close your eyes, become aware of your surroundings, sense them. Feeling comfortable all the time.

Listen to your breathing, feel that air going in and out of your lungs. Feel the air around you. Become "aware".

Do this for a few minutes.

Open your eyes and look out of that window again. Now what do you see? – look closer. Do you notice the difference?

Before there was for example a tree, now there is a beautiful tall tree, with leaves of green that are glinting in the sun. The sun is shining through the branches. Notice the colour of the trunk and the shapes, the birds flitting amongst the branches, the clouds that are sitting on top of the tree in a beautiful painted picture setting.

That's a bit different from just seeing the tree. OK so it may be raining when you look out of your window and it may not be a tree you are looking at, but you get the idea. Look deeply at what you are missing. We do this every day of our lives. Such a shame. Try doing this more frequently and see how more beautiful the world around you is.

Exercise 2

Sitting quietly again close your eyes. Imagine you are looking at a blackboard. Pick up a piece of chalk – which is at the bottom of the board – and write on the board. Write your name. Rub it out – you now have a clean board again. Draw a tree and a house and a dog – or whatever you want to draw. Finished – now rub it all out.

See what you have done, you have created an image in your head, you created the blackboard, you saw it, and then you put something on it, and then rubbed it out.

If you have difficulty with this, keep trying. This visualisation ability is going to be a great help if you are to develop your skills as a medium.

Once we have learned how to focus the mind, we can then invite spirit to draw close to us. This process can vary so much from one person to the next and some people will find it easier than others. Don't worry about this. It will come with time and practice.

We have to learn how to invite spirit in and also how to ask spirit to leave (the opening up and closing down process). The reason we do this is that otherwise we would be bombarded by spirit all the time and we would get no peace. It is important to point out here that we have a physical life to lead and we can invite spirit in from time to time if we wish. Spirit also get very excited when they know they have a willing open channel to work with, but you must get a sort of mutual respect or pact with spirit.

Exercise 3

We all have guides and helpers working with us all the time. Sit quietly with your eyes closed. Become aware of your breathing. Breath in and out slowly. When you feel ready "ask" one of your guides to step forward.

Remember if at any time you are not happy with what is happening, ask them to go away. You are doing this with love so you will get love back. Your helpers will be there and willing to show themselves.

Imagine that face building up in front of you. Look closely at the nose, the eyes, the shape of them, the colour. What nationality would you say they were? Look at the wrinkles, lines, crevices in the face. Is it a male or female? Are they young or old? You may have to keep practicing but do keep trying.

I have been doing this exercise myself very recently and it is incredible how they show themselves. Almost like a "mug shot". They look at me full face, then turn from side to side, so I can see all the contours and shapes and marks. Its amazing. Now they come in so fast and its one after the other. They are just as excited to show themselves to me as I am to see them.

Exercise 4

Again, sit with your eyes closed. Quietly become aware of your breathing. When you feel ready ask a member of your family who has passed to show themselves to you. Look deep in to their eyes, watch what they are doing. Now "listen", what do you hear. Keep trying. The more you do these type of exercises in the early stages the easier it will be for you when you are linking to spirit later on.

Being a medium is about being able to connect with spirit and give messages from loved ones who have passed. We have to give information to the recipient about the person from spirit that will prove categorically that we have their relative there.

I meet so many people who are leading this life by spirit, expecting and asking all the time for spirit to make their decisions for them and not realising that we have a physical life that we have to experience. They realise, and we should too, that we can ask them for help, but we must not blame them every time something goes wrong. We have freedom of choice. Spirit will try and help us when they can and we can always ask them for help, but we must also realise that this is our earthly life so choices are made and sometimes they may be wrong. Sometimes though we ARE given the right information and help from spirit but we don't always listen, which is a different thing altogether.

So let's start off at the beginning!

Like anything new we learn we have to study the basics which can be tedious and boring but we have do to this.
Please remember this is <u>NOT</u> an overnight process. You have to have a complete understanding of what you are doing. You are dealing with people's emotions at all times and therefore you are not allowed to meddle or predict or give information about bad situations to come. We are NOT fortune tellers.

We are people who have been given a gift to communicate with the spirit world and our job, is to prove that life is continual, there is no death.

So you have this curiosity, wondering is there something else out there, can I do it...

How DO we do it?

Lets get started...

Preparation

Firstly we need to be aware and accept that we have a physical AND a spiritual body which work alongside one another. The physical body is the vehicle we need to carry us through this earthly life and is obviously solid. The spiritual body however vibrates at a higher level and cannot as such be "seen". It is an energy force.

We need to know that when someone passes to spirit we can communicate with them in the spirit world.

People should also remember that you do not have to be a medium to be able to link to your loved ones in spirit, we can all "listen" to spirit for ourselves.

Know and trust that this energy is with us, here and now, and that our spirit and that of our guides, helpers and loved ones can help us at all times.

There is no death just another dimension that we have to learn to tap into.

We should also know that spirit are not there to cause us harm, they are spirits who want to work with us or are the spirits of people who would have cared for us when they were physically here and that they still want to be able to do that for us every day. They are there for us, to comfort us, help us and guide us as best they can. What is there to be afraid of? When we need help or guidance or answers, just ask. They are listening and they want to help.

Spirit have obviously got the better of your curiosity so far and you need to know that your teaching guides will work with you, at your pace, and direct you in the best way they can. They will often direct you to the field of mediumship they think best for you, which might not be what you think is best for you. But trust what they are doing and how they are working with you. Trust is the most important part of this whole process of learning to connect (communicate) with them.

What are Chakras/Psychic Centres?

"In yoga vortices that penetrate the body and the body's aura, through which various energies, including the universal life force, are received, transformed, and distributed. Chakras are believed to play a vital role in physical, mental and emotional health and in spiritual development".

The word 'chakra' is derived from a Sanskrit word meaning 'wheel'; but perhaps even a better translation would be spinning wheel. If you could see chakras you would be able to see each chakra as a spinning vortex or wheel of energy.

These are the energy points of our spiritual body. It is important to realise that if our spiritual body is not in line with our physical body we will not function correctly. We will have dis-ease! So we need to make sure that our spiritual and physical bodies are balanced and in sync with one another. We can do this by balancing or "firing up" as I like to call it, our Chakra points. There are 7 main chakra points:

Name of Chakra	Colour	Position	Function
Base or Root	Red	Groin Area	Grounding
Sacral	Orange	Approx 2" below the navel	Emotional connection
Solar Plexus	Yellow	Upper stomach	Self esteem
Heart	Pink/Green	Over the heart	love centre of our human energy system
Throat	Blue	Bottom of the throat	Communication
Third Eye	Purple	Middle of the forehead	The 'eye' to the spirit world, allowing us to 'see' spirit
Crown	White	Top of the head	Chakra point we open when we want to 'communicate' with spirit

Energising these points and making sure that they are functioning properly is very easy to do and so beneficial to us.

Exercise 5

Firstly, starting at the base/root chakra, which is in the groin area, imagine the colour as a Catherine Wheel. Imagine/visualise that you have just lit the touch paper and then watch as it starts to spin faster and faster and as it does so the colour intensifies. "Feel" and imagine the energy that exudes from this. If you had a difficulty with doing this then just "know" that that is what is happening.

Work your way up through the chakra points doing the same for each one.

Sacral Chakra – Orange
Solar Plexus - Yellow
Heart – Green
Throat – Blue
Third Eye – Purple
Crown - White

Exercise 6

When you have energised your chakra points, you could now imagine a fine silver thread starting at the Base Chakra and threading its way through all the individual points in turn and then out of the Crown Chakra. When you have got to this point imagine you are able to pull the thread tight which aligns all the chakra points.

Once you have learned how to energise these points you will be in a better position to be able to "listen" to your inner self and be a better link to the spirit world. The reason for this is that you have reawakened, or opened your spiritual body.

This is a great exercise to do as a meditation, and is very calming and eventually you will feel more and more energised in yourself. Choose some very relaxing music, a quiet room, and enjoy.

Always remember your imagination is the best thing you have been blessed with especially for working with spirit, and especially at the beginning when you are learning to develop – so use it.

Chakra points should always be energised. You need your spiritual body to be open, functioning properly and working in line with your physical body.

You will learn later on about "opening up" and "closing down" to spirit in order for communication between us and them. This is a different process and for a different reason. Chakra points should always be "firing on all cylinders". I have heard people say that when you "close down" you should close the chakras. I would disagree with this. At this stage you are not "open" to or "working with" spirit.

If you are fairly new to spiritual work you will be unknowingly more susceptible to the energies around you. You won't understand why you are feeling tired, drained, sad, emotional. This can be quite draining. What is happening basically is that you are an open channel. Spirit get very excited when they find a new channel to work through. If you imagine that we are like beacons of light to the spirit world and some shine brighter than others. When spirit find a brighter beacon, one who can potentially work closely with them, they get excited like when we find a new friend and want to be with them all the time.

For example you could be in a supermarket, imagine all those people, all those energies, all those spirits. They see you as an open channel and think "hey we have found someone we can communicate with" and they will. So you need to protect yourself from this constant unwanted bombardment from them. You and spirit need to realise that there is a time and a place for communication. You have to be firm with them and yourself.

Exercise 7

The Protective Bubble

Imagine yourself stepping into a giant bubble, make sure you close it or zip it up. This is your protection from outside influences. The bubble creates a protective space around you. Any attempts to communicate will bounce off you or just go over the top!

This is also a good exercise to do if you feel that you are going into a situation that you are uncomfortable with; are placed into a difficult environment, or around people you are uncomfortable with.

If I get an immediate sense of an uncomfortable energy with my visitors, I wrap my bubble around me. I also use this technique. If I have to go into a potentially difficult meeting I put that bubble around me AND ask spirit to help me! It always works – try it.

Remember your spiritual body and your physical body have to be working together. Within your bubble the spiritual body/Chakras are protected.

The Aura

"An envelope of vital energy, which apparently radiates from everything in nature: minerals, plants, animals and humans. The aura is not visible to normal vision, but may be seen by clairvoyance as a halo of light. Then it often appears as a multi-coloured mist that fades off into sparks, rays and streamers."

We know that we are made up of energy. We have an energy field (aura) around us. Some people have the ability to actually see this aura. Hopefully in time you will be able to do this also but don't worry if you can't, for the time being it's not that important.

However for the moment, I just want you to imagine and know that it is there. Liken it to the cereal advert on TV where the children have had their breakfast and leave the house with a white glow around them. This is the energy field I am talking about, and what it looks like.

The aura is a reflection of who and what we are physically and spiritually. Some people will also have the ability to see colours in the aura. This may come later for you. Healers are able to use this function to be able to "see" what is wrong with a person. Our ill health shows up in our aura. Many healers are reported to see "dips" in the aura over a person's head, or dull colours, which is an indication of problems with the person's health, the colours being related to certain parts of the body.

I should point out at this stage that not all psychic exercises work for everyone. Similarly my way of describing how to do an exercise may not be quite right for you so if you feel you are not getting it, try it a slightly different way. This is what I have learned to do over the years. Generally get the gist of an exercise, and then tweak it slightly to suit yourself.

Your imagination is the best thing you could have as a developing medium. Being able to create pictures in your mind, like daydreaming, you are seeing pictures, but you know that they are not "really" there.

Guided meditation allows you to use your imagination to see things that the guide is putting to you and is certainly very good practice.

Some of us have logical thinking brains and so it may be more difficult to trust these images, but do give it a try.

Its not just us humans who have an aura, in fact every living thing has one. If we look closely enough we should be able to see it. Why not have a go now? Always remember to ask permission first.

Exercise 8

Choose something that is living around you. This could be the cat, your friend, or even a plant. Concentrate on a spot slightly off centre to them or it, almost like daydreaming but you are still seeing the person. Let your eyes and mind relax and watch what happens. You should start to see a milky white "shadow" of the person. You may not be able to do this straight away, but keep practicing and it will work.

A few years ago there was something called "magic eye picture" books, where all that was on the page was a complete mix of colours and shapes when you looked at it. However you had to take your focus "off" the picture to be able to see what was "in" the picture. Well this is the same sort of principle.

"Many things in life are just the same! Looked at in one way, they just don't make sense. Try it the other way round."...anon

Learning to feel and see this energy field will help you a great deal in understanding mediumship. When I first started being able to do this I was amazed. Keep practicing.

We can also feel the aura, try this exercise.

Exercise 9

Sit opposite a friend and get them to put their hands, palms flat and facing you, then you do the same. You and your partner bringing your hands slowly together towards each other. What do you feel? You may have to try this a few times, but you should get a tingling or a pushing sensation. When you have "got it" then try again and you will find that you can bring your hands further back and still feel that energy. You are actually "feeling" your partner's energy field.

Again you can do this with any living object.

Exercise 10

Try practicing this on yourself. Bring the palms of your hands together, or bring your palms towards or around your head and feel the pressure as you feel your own aura.

The more you practice this the easier it becomes and the more you will become aware of that energy field around people and things and of course yourself.

Exercise 11

Trees are powerful energy sources. My friends laugh at me when I go tree hugging. You can either "hug" the tree trunk, just touch it, or just stand on the roots, whatever way you do it, you will never know how powerful it is unless you try. Remember every living thing has an energy field around it that we can "feel" or "sense" – try it.

When we try to communicate with spirit we are linking our energy field with the energy field of the spirit communicator. If we are aware of how our own energy field feels then this will make it easier for us to become aware of when spirit has come in to our aura. When we "ask" spirit to draw close to us we are trying to link or overlap the two energies and allow ourselves to feel, sense and hear.

So practicing these first few exercises is quite important.

Psychic, Clairvoyant, Medium
What is the difference?

There often seems to be much confusion over the definitions between Psychics, Mediums and Clairvoyants.

Psychic
Defined as pertaining to mental forces, telepathy, extra sensory perception. Psychics have a 'mind connection' with you and will also read your energy field, so they pick up on your thoughts and energy most of all.

Clair
Then there are a number of 'clair' abilities but the three that most people will have heard of are Clairvoyance, Clairaudience and Clairsentience.

Clairvoyance – clear seeing
Defined as the ability to see things beyond our normal senses. Clairvoyance actually translates to 'clear seeing'. It means that the person that is working with their clairvoyant ability will be able to see images of people, places or things in their minds eye. They will usually to be able to describe to you what they are seeing during a reading or giving a message. It does not mean that they are fortune tellers. That doesn't mean that you won't get information about the future, but clairvoyance by definition just simply means, clear seeing, and not necessarily, seeing the future. A good clairvoyant will, and indeed should, validate things for you that have happened in the past and things that are happening in the present. If they don't, how will you know or believe if what they are saying about the future holds any weight?

Clairaudience – clear hearing
This means that we will hear information from Spirit. This might be one's own Spirit Guides or if working as a Medium giving messages it will be the spirit of the loved one that is no longer here, giving that information. Most will hear this as a voice in their head as if talking with oneself.

Clairsentience – clear sensing

This is where we feel things, or sense things. This often comes, working as a medium, when someone has passed with a certain illness or condition. For a split second you feel a sensation that they would have felt before they passed or a condition they would have suffered with during their life. Feeling that pain or sensation enables you to describe this to the person you are giving the message to. This often helps to validate which particular person is coming through from Spirit for them.

This sensing could also be relating to the person sitting in front of you. Was it spirit that hurt their leg or was it the person for whom the message is intended?

And then sometimes you just "know" something - one of my lovely teachers said there should be Clair-knowing which says what it means!

Mediumship

Defined as contacting and being able to communicate with spirits of the dead. The more complex definition is that a medium is the 'channel' by which information from spirit passes to the living or in more general terms the channel through which any energy-passes. By this definition all of us are mediums. This is because we all channel energy to some degree or another.

If we draw, we are a medium (as is the pencil) through which energy flows to create the picture on the page. If we sing, we are a medium (as is the voice) through which energy flows to create a song. If we are healers (another topic entirely) we are mediums through which the energy flows to our clients and so on.. .

This then means by its very nature anyone working with spirit or energy on any level could be called a medium. A medium in this sense, is then being defined as a 'channel'.

So someone that calls themselves a Clairvoyant/Medium, by rights, should for example, be able to describe your loved ones from the spirit world and also to describe visually things around your home or family. However, there are a few 'clairvoyant/mediums' out there that aren't in fact either of these! They may 'cold read' people, but might be reading via their psychic or sentient ability and not actually 'seeing' anything at all, or indeed they may not be able to talk with your loved ones in spirit either.

As a sitter, never be afraid to ask your 'reader' how they work, they should always be happy to explain it to you. This way, you know what sort of reading you can expect.

Armed with this knowledge we should now be able to get to the next stage of preparing ourselves and learning to access that "higher self".

Mediums have the ability to be able to do the above objectively (pictures forming in the mind or mind's eye) and subjectively (actually physically being able to "see" spirit).

Apparently being able to link to our higher self uses a frontal lobe of the brain, which is in the forehead area. Something that I only discovered recently. What I have known for a long time is that we use the "third eye" which is also supposedly located in the mid-forehead area.

It is important to remember that all mediums are psychic but not all psychics are mediums.

Recognising your Potential

"Mediuimship is an ancient and universal practice, undertaken to commune with the divine prophesy, communicate with spirits of the dead, perform paranormal feats, and challenge the universal life force for healing".

The job of a medium has always been to prove that when the physical body dies, the spirit lives on. Having learnt to "feel" energy around ourselves and other living things, the next stage is to learn how to "feel" when spirit are close to us.

We have this energy field around us and so do spirit. What we are hoping to achieve next is to ask spirit to draw closc to us. What will happen then will be an overlapping of these two energy fields/auras, giving us the ability to sense/hear/feel spirit.

To start with, sensing spirit can be difficult. You will ask yourselves so many questions. Is it real, am I making it up, is it my imagination? I had all the same questions, even though I had been seeing spirit from a young age. When I started classes in order to focus this, I still sometimes thought my mind was playing tricks on me. The other thing I hear from people, especially if you are working with others, "am I going to make a fool out of myself". Well please do understand that all mediums, no matter who they are or how good they are, will have all had to go through these same dilemmas. I for one continue to question all the time, I never take for granted the abilities that I have.

I always say that you should trust the information you are getting, and believe it is not you or your mind or your own thoughts. Trust that spirit are wanting to work with us and we have to go along with it.

I usually ask my students why have they been drawn to learn about spirit, what do they need to learn and why do they want to communicate.

They don't always know themselves. Sometimes we are just "chosen". I explain that to the spirit we are all like beacons of light that they can see from the spirit world and some of us shine brighter than others. Its the ones who shine brighter that spirit realise they can work with easier, are better channels for them, and these are the ones they choose to work with.

I believe spirit are looking for as many good channels to work with as possible and I believe this is in order to help the world we live in and to help people in general. Giving people more positivity and for more people to realise that there is more to life than just our earthly existence, thereby giving people more hope and comfort.

When you first start working with spirit it will sometimes seem like such an upward struggle. Then at other times it will be amazing and you will be going great guns. Don't ever be disheartened. You will be continually tested by spirit to see if you are good enough. What way is best for them to work with you? Do you have the dedication necessary and of course is your intention true?

I remember when I first started development classes and first sensing spirit, it seemed like such a long drawn out process. I would get the sense of a person with me who was giving me information, but it was me seeing/ sensing, working out in my own mind and then translating the information, that took the time and the effort.

Remember we cannot get it all right when we are starting.

Another thing to remember is that our interpretation of information given to us is not necessarily correct and this is another learning process. What do the images we are seeing mean to/for us. And for each person they will be different. For example I would ask spirit to draw close to me, then get a sense of is it a male or female energy with me. Then ask for a description i.e. height, age, hair, build, jobs, hobbies, where they lived, married, how many children, how they passed and so on. In time this "asking" will stop and you will find that it will be an automatic process of knowing. You will just speak without having to work things out, but will "know" that they are there with you and are giving you the relevant information.

Opening up and closing down to spirit

"Speak to Him, thou, for He hears, and Spirit with Spirit can meet – closer is He than breathing, and nearer than hands or feet"... Alfred, Lord Tennyson

This is an important part of your work. To be able to work with and link to spirit we need to be "open". It is equally important to remember that when we are NOT working with them we need to be "closed". We have to, if you like, build up a respect between ourselves and spirit about the work we are going to be doing for and with them! So they need to know when they can communicate with us and when not to.

As I have mentioned previously, if we are continually an open channel, this can be so draining and tiring. We need to have a balance between the two worlds. So please when you open up to spirit, always remember when you are finished, to close down.

Many people have different ways of doing this. Some will sit and meditate for a while, sitting in a quiet room before working with spirit.

I have never been comfortable with this myself, mainly because as I am usually running late and then literally having to get up on platform and "work". But it is good practice to try and still the mind and be able to prepare to work.

When I first started doing platform, I remember how scared I was and I could not believe how hard my head and heart pounded with fear and how "noisy" that was. I basically told spirit that they had to quieten me down in order for me to work, so that I could listen to the information they were giving me. It worked, what I had actually done was TRUST spirit completely, to use me as a channel for them.

We need to be able to quieten our minds and start to become aware of ALL the things that are going on around us AND within us. We talk about our intuition, if we tapped in to our intuitive thoughts and trusted more of these thoughts we would be able to make better more informed decisions.

For the time being I am going to ask you to just TRUST that if you are meant to be doing this work, they (spirit) will be there.

Ask to open or link and ask to close or break the link.

Linking to spirit

At this point I would ask you to go back over the chapter on energising the chakra points. Page 60

When you have done all of them, at the crown chakra point, imagine that you have a little trap door on the top of your head and you are going to open it in order for spirit to come close to us. You are inviting them in.

Remember never be frightened about what is happening as at any point you can close this trap door and ask spirit to go away. Also if you are doing this with the right intentions – wanting to prove that life is eternal – then you will always be safe. Remember that they will respect your requests.

In all the years I have personally been involved with working for spirit, I have never come across an evil spirit or for that matter a spirit that didn't listen when I told them to go away. This is the mutual respect, you listen and they will listen. You may have to ask them more than once, but they will listen.

Remember the bubble of energy/aura that surrounds each of us. We are going to ask spirit to come close to us in order to communicate. So the energy field around both you and spirit are going to overlap. This overlapping of energy is where the information is going to come from and how we are going to be able to "communicate" with them.

Always remember to trust whatever information you get. The most bizarre information you get, may be bizarre to you but could be so relative to your recipient, so give it.

When you ask spirit to draw close to you, your guides and helpers will be there working with you too. I realised early on that some of my guides/helpers were actually relatives. This was a great comfort to me in the beginning and still is today.

We are going to be asking and listening and then "seeing" what comes back to us. The translating of the information received can sometimes be difficult as you will be given signs, symbols, words. More on this a little later on.

People often ask why don't spirit just say "my name is ... I lived at ... and I am ... relative" it doesn't always work like that. Sometimes spirit are learning to communicate themselves, they may not have been good communicators when they were on earth, or they may have had a physical problem here which made it impossible to communicate. Even the best mediums do not always get information in such a precise way, then some do. But if we don't it could be us not feeling right on the day, the recipient/ audience not being so open or friendly, a whole number of reasons. Today you may get your information in a precise way and tomorrow you may not. There are so many factors which change this process and you have to work with whatever way spirit want to work with you on the day. I am constantly being challenged by the fact that they change this process so frequently. This way you can never become complacent with this work.

Remember this is an amazing skill/gift. I still get so excited about the fact that I can do this work AND its fun. You should always do this work with love in your heart and a smile on your face – makes it so much easier. Once you stop feeling like that stop doing it! Initially spirit will look at how best to work with you. You may not end up a working platform medium. Some of you won't even want that anyway. At the beginning of my development, spirit worked with me on mediumship, psychometry, trance and automatic writing. I think that no matter what you want to end up doing, spirit will have the last say, but it is important to try everything, whatever opportunity opens up for you try it.

It can also be a long process, please be patient, Rome didn't get built in a day! And in general mediumship doesn't happen overnight. You need to go through the motions and there will be many pitfalls along the way and many learning curves, some steep and some not so, but you just have to go with what they think is right for you and not the other way around.

We have asked spirit to draw close to us and we have opened up – believe they are there.

I liken this next step to walking in to a bar! You walk in and you can see people. You walk up to one person in order to start communicating/talking. Visually you could describe their appearance, i.e. how tall, short, dark/blonde hair, or no hair at all, fat, thin, the way they dress, glasses etc. This is what we are going to do with spirit. We have to be able to identify our spirit communicator in sufficient detail that our recipient is able to identify the giver of the message. Try taking your focus off the person you are working with. Like the Magic Eye Pictures or day dreaming. It makes it easier to "see".

When you are asking for information from spirit, I think it is easier to ask a question in your mind and quickly give the first answer that comes into your head. This is the best way to work, as this gives less time for your own mind to come in to play, and to question what you are "getting".

Students start off sensing spirit, then they start with their questions, they ask and then they wait. I can see they are having such a battle in their own minds about the information/answers being received. "Did I make that up", "that was something I heard/saw today", "that sounds like my Grandma", blah blah. Again trust and believe in spirit and yourselves.

It is easier when starting off to use a set format which will be a series of questions to ascertain who we are communicating with in order that your recipient/sitter will be able to recognise who we are talking to. As you get more experienced you won't need these questions, spirit will just put this information into your mind.

To start with, if you give out 10 bits of information using this quick response format, you will find that most of the information is correct.

At the initial stages don't worry if you don't get it all right, it will come with time, practice and experience.

I was taught by a formula called CERT:

C	Communicator
E	Evidence
R	Reason for coming
T	Tie up your message

If you follow this method you will always work correctly – you will always be CERTain.

It is important for your recipient to "know" that they are getting a message from their particular family member and that this family member is categorically identified and not just a random message. It is also important in a public arena that the audience "know" this to be the case.

Who is giving that information, where is it coming from? If we don't have that recognition we could be seen to be cold reading, mind reading, psychically reading. You need this proof and so does your recipient.

Working as a medium, you are a sensitive, so you may be very sensitive to criticism. Don't leave yourself open for that criticism. Be true to yourself, to spirit, and of course to your sitter.

Most people come for a reading as they are wanting to know that their loved one in spirit is still with them and that they are OK, out of pain, helping them and still loves them. Therefore every time we connect with spirit we must work out who is communicating with us.

If we work this way we are working on a "spirit" level. Just giving information and not identifying your communicator means you will be working on a "psychic" level. If you work with spirit it is so much easier as they are giving you the information directly, whereas if you work on a psychic level you are trying to pull the information from the energies around your sitter.

Once you are able to give a description of how they looked you then need to be nosy and ask them questions about themselves.

List of suggested questions –
Remember you've just met them and your being nosey!

Is the energy I am sensing :

Male or female?
Tall or short?
Build?
Have any distinguishing features?
Fat?
Thin?
Age?
Where they lived?
Type of house?
> Ask them to show you inside the house.

Clean, tidy, messy?
Married?
Family around them?
Number of children?
Hobbies?
Work they did?
> Do they show their hands or a collar and tie?

How did they die?
> If you scan your own body and ask that question, you should be able to "feel" their pain or reason for dying.

What part of the country or world did they come from ?
> Picture a map in your mind and let them direct you to where they were from.

What sort of personality did they have?

Delve into their personalities, even if they were a miserable or grouchy person when here, that information could be the defining factor as far as your recipient is concerned, so give it.

Remember that working – no matter what work – with fun and laughter raises the energies/vibrations and you will work better.

What you are trying to do here is to build up a picture of the person that is linking with you. This has to be done in such a way that your recipient/sitter is absolutely 100% sure of that connection and who that person from spirit is.

Exercise 12

Step 1
Make sure that you are in a quiet environment

Start by doing some deep breathing, concentrating on the breath going in and out of your body.

Step 2
Energise your Chakra points (refer to page 60)

You can also try doing this with some nice relaxing music playing in the background, this usually helps you to focus and concentrate.

Make sure you have your phone switched off. Unnecessary interruptions and sudden noises break concentration and will distract you from what you are trying to do.

At the point where our spiritual body is working in line with our physical body we are ready to invite spirit in. Once again, remember the energy field/aura around us.

We are inviting spirit in to our energy field – and these energy fields are overlapping . Like the feeling in the exercise about energy (page 64) the physical energy of our partner or ourselves, when spirit enter this energy field we will be able to "feel" this also.

Step 3

Imagine that you have a trap door on the top of your head, at the crown chakra point. We are going to allow this to open and we are going to ask spirit to come close to us. We are, if you like, giving them permission to communicate/link with us in order for us to work together. Never be afraid or feel uncomfortable when you do this, if at any time you feel uncomfortable you can always close the trap door – "close down" and ask spirit to step back.

To start with, being able to sense spirit may be difficult and you may find yourself trying to determine if it is "you", or are you making it up? Please, at this stage TRUST. We have opened that trap door and we have given permission to connect. KNOW and TRUST that they are there.

Step 4

Get a sense of whether this spirit communicator is a male or a female energy. Follow the list of questions set out earlier in this section (page 81).

The more experience we get, as with most things we learn to do, the easier this will become. When I started, spirit would give me an idea of it is was male or female by the way they made me feel. A male, may made me feel big and strong and a female, soft and gentle.

Step 5

Now we have to get nosey, remember the bar environment! You can see what they look like, now it is time to ask them about themselves and get some more detailed information.

Quick fire questions are always a good idea as this will not give you the chance to change or misinterpret the information you are being given by your spirit communicator. It will be as they give it.

Ask your question and go with the first answer that pops in to your head, initial thoughts are always the best to go with.

At this stage you may not get all the information right. Don't let that fluster you for the moment you will find that out of 10 bits of information you receive, only a few bits are possibly going to be wrong. This could be because of inexperience, misinterpretation, or many other factors. In time this will improve.

Step 6
So we have a male/female and we start asking questions. You may wish to refer to the list on page 81.

Remember it is like walking into a room and meeting someone for the first time. You can give a description of the person, because you are looking at them. With mediumship, you may not SEE physically, you may just get a sense, or a feeling, or pictures in your head. Remember the clair's (clairvoyance, clairsentience, clairaudience, page 67). You must also be aware that you can get this information subjectively or objectively, i.e. in your head or physically in front of you "seeing" it.

Whatever way spirit work with you, just trust. This statement to trust is repeated often in this book because it is so important. Once I had learned to trust 100% in my connections and the information I was getting, I improved ten-fold.

Spirit may change the way they work with you, I think this is so you do not become complacent with them or your work. Every time I work it changes in some way, so please don't be put off.

Your spirit communicators may also give you pictures, of things that are familiar to you. For example they may give you a picture of YOUR Grandad, when you have the grandad of your recipient trying to connect with you. They may also give you other things that would be familiar to you, perhaps a person you know of the same build, age, or personality to your spirit communicator.

Step 7

You now have this spirit person close to you and he/she is giving you a description of themselves. Now look at other things they may show you.

If I get shown a ring, I ask or look to see, does the ring have a stone, if yes what colour. So does the ring indicate a wedding ring, an engagement ring, a dress ring, then you may ask, what is the significance of them showing you a ring. This could indicate a forthcoming marriage. Are they taking the ring off the finger? This could indicate a marriage break up.

If you are, for instance, shown a book, don't be satisfied with just being shown a book, ask to be shown what the book is about. Look at the cover.

If you are given an indication of an illness in the chest area, ask them to indicate is it the heart or the lungs?

Be as pushy and as nosey as you like, they want to work with you the same as you with them. In the initial stages, I would suggest that you continue to push for specific evidence. This is important. You can go on to give messages at a later stage. It is so important that you learn to give the specific information so as to be absolutely sure that your recipient knows who you are communicating with from the spirit world.

I know the message from a loved one is just as important but you have to make sure that you both know who you are communicating with.

You may get a name. Don't fall in to the trap of 'I have a J name' and then reel off a whole load of 'J' names! That is making things fit and it is not good practice. Ask for the name and wait for your answer, they may just give you a single letter. At that point don't go through a list, just say "I have a name beginning with the letter .....". That will be good enough and will be more evidential.

If you are given anniversaries, birthday, passing, or wedding anniversary, ask them (spirit) to show you a calendar and look at the numbers. Or just ask them what date in the month and listen.

When giving information to a recipient be aware that they can't always remember information at the time, they may have a "mental block" and it's not until they go away and think of what has been said that the penny drops. If your recipient does not understand a piece of information, go back to spirit and ask them again. If the information is given again in a similar way, then stick with it.

It could just be that your interpretation of that piece of information is wrong. Ask spirit to give it another way, a way in which your recipient will totally understand what is being given.

Step 8

When you have given all your information and your spirit communicator has left you, you must remember to "close down". Do this by closing the trap door at the crown chakra point, which you opened up to start with.

This is very important, as you don't want spirits communicating with you all the time, which can be very draining etc. If you are "open" all the time, you will have all sorts of spirits talking to you constantly. You need to protect your physical/spiritual body from continual bombardment from spirit. Remember to say thank you to spirit and your helpers / guides for working with you. Always be respectful of them.

Once you feel comfortable and happy with the information you are giving about spirit communicators and your recipients are convinced, only then would I suggest moving on to give messages.

The message IS important but in the initial stages the student has to learn to receive, interpret and give specific precise information. This is the information that will get your spirit communicator recognised by your recipient/sitter. I think this is the crux of what we are doing, proving.

Exercise 13

There are different ways of beginning. Another option is when you have energised all the chakra points and you get to the final point which is the crown, open the trap door as before but this time let the white light expand from this chakra point, and allow it to drizzle over your body and fill your auric field.

Then imagine that white light spreading outwards into the room around you. What you have done basically is you have expanded your energy field and have created a larger "overlap". This may make it easier for you to be able to link to spirit, allowing you to perhaps create a stronger link.

Try this and then try linking again and see what a difference it makes.

You may have to ask spirit to draw close to you more than once during the initial stages as you may actually feel that spirit are drifting "in and out". This is quite normal.

I hear people saying all the time, "oh they've gone now". They haven't necessarily. Sometimes students, especially at the beginning, just get a bit frightened. They don't want to look silly, or are struggling to get information, so they give up too easily. They may just be trying too hard and battling in their heads – I have done this myself. But once you have made your connection to spirit, know that they are there. Just ask them to step closer to you and then "feel" this.

Repeat steps 4 – 8 inclusive from the previous exercise.

You will find that many of us have similar people who have been in our lives. For instance a Nan, that liked cooking, that had back problems, short curly permed hair and wore glasses. But how many Nan's would have had a wooden leg, false eye, only wore a wig, walked with a walking frame, danced around with a feather boa, played Bingo on Thursdays, was on the way to the shops to buy something specific the day they died!

These are the bits of evidence that you need. I have had all of these and these silly little bits were the crunch point where someone says, "well only I/she would have known that".

The most bizarre or trivial thing to you could be so relevant to your reading. This is what you are looking for, this is why working on the specific precise evidence is SO important, and will make you a great medium. When someone has been to you for a reading, they will go away and say "wow how did they know that". That's what you have to aim for.

Basically don't be satisfied with just being "shown" something, ask why, what is the significance. And make sure you get the answer as this could be so important to the recipient.

DON'T try and analyse what you are getting. Our job is to give the information and the recipient is the one to analyse. So many times when I do readings, the information comes so quickly and I don't have time to get an explanation of what I am seeing. Afterwards when you have finished the reading, then you can speak to the sitter and they can explain.

Exercise 14

In a group class, get someone to stand in front of the class to work as the medium, they are to have their back to the rest of the group.

Get the whole class to stand up.

The medium is to get a connection to spirit. Then give the information a piece at a time. Members of the group who do not recognise the information are to sit down.

You will find that the last person standing will be who the message is for.

Exercise 15

Pre-cognative reading

This is a reading that is done in advance.

If you know you have a class coming up, sit quietly and ask spirit to draw close to you. Tell them that you want to do a reading for someone who will be at class on a given date. Just sit and wait and see what comes to you. You will be surprised.

The first time I did this was at the Arthur Findlay College and I was so shocked that so much of the information was accurate.

A few days after this course I was doing a public demonstration of mediumship with my good friend Martin Parsons, and I thought I would give this a try. I sat quietly before the event and connected to spirit and asked for a message. Well I wrote three pages!

At the demonstration I stood up and said what I had done, and said I would read out the first three bits of information and see how it went. Well after the third bit no one put their hand up. So I screwed up the piece of paper and threw it on the floor. I carried on with my demonstration and proceeded to start giving a message to a lady in the audience. When I had given the first few bits of information I realised that what I was telling her was on my piece of paper! So I picked up the piece of paper, unravelled it and again went over the first three bits of information and guess what, she understood it all.

Interpreting or Translating information

The ability to interpret is sometimes more valuable than a literal statement of what is seen clairvoyantly. Spirit will often use symbolism to get their messages across to you. They will give pictures of items, and as a medium you have to try and interpret what that symbol means.

Translating information can sometimes be difficult, but again with time and practice you will work out what these symbols mean to you. It will be different for each one of you.

There is a three way thing going on, you, spirit and your sitter. You and your sitter may have a different interpretation of an object / picture. For instance you may see a pair of scissors. This could mean that maybe there is a need for cutting ties, or it could simply be that the person we are communicating with from spirit was a hairdresser or used scissors in their job, or that could be related to the sitter.

If say we interpret this as cutting ties, and we get an answer of "no" from our sitter, don't be put off. Stay calm and simply go back and ask spirit to give you that information in a way that the sitter WILL understand. Often students when they get a "no" go in to a panic or get flustered, and say "I can't do this" or "I'm not getting this, I'm no good". Rubbish! No's are great. Look on a no as a challenge. Go back to spirit and work out what it DOES mean, they will work with you and give you what you need. Never be thrown in this way. In a training situation you have the time to do this, remain calm and ask away.

Spirit will always do this, and will work with you. Always know that information you are being given from spirit is correct, it's usually just our interpretation that could be wrong. So we have to work this out. Again it comes down to time and practice. We must make sure that we don't put our interpretation on something. Again, learn to trust spirit and that they will give us the correct information and we will get our message across to our sitter.

It is sometimes confusing when our sitter has their own interpretation of our evidence and again we need to be certain in our trust of spirit. I find that sometimes a sitter is so engrossed or emotional that they don't understand certain information. I have known many times I have had this happen. I know that the information I am getting from spirit is correct so it's great when people come back to you and confirm that you were right.

When I first started doing sittings on my own, I did a session with a lady and for a whole hour and she just kept saying no. I thought "I was rubbish" and should "pack it all in" and "why was I doing this", "what was going on"! The following day she rang me to tell me she had played the tape to her dad who had said yes, to all the information. I think spirit were testing me big time that day. But I am still here and working with them.

If you are CERTain that the information you have been given is correct, stick with it. I know I keep repeating this but it is so important with this work that you know it will come with practice and experience and you will learn in time what is right and what is not. You will sometimes just "know" what you are giving is correct.

It is not always easy to translate or interpret the information you are getting from spirit. A lot of people ask why spirit don't give exact information, in that "I have a man here, his name is, his age is and he lived at…." I suppose if you think about it ,when you are talking to people in this world you don't always get a straight answer to questions, or someone else's explanation about something may not be quite to our understanding. I believe it's the same with communication with spirit.

Look at some things that I have been given as symbols. How would you interpret these?

Scissors
> cutting ties; sewing; hairdressing;

Clock/time
> the timing of something; memory of a clock/watch; the time on the watch/clock could indicate the time of passing;

Tree
> growth; tree of life; roots; progress;

House
> Home; stability; move; relationship;

Cross or crossroads
> crossroads; indecision; which direction to go in; religion;

Spanner
> problems with car; spanner in the works; difficulties; mechanic

Car
> transport; travel; new car; movement

Monkey
> impish, foreign connection; or just a monkey!

Garden shears
> gardener, cutting ties, your garden needs doing!

Each of us will have a different explanation for the same symbol. So a bit of a minefield really. But please don't be disheartened. It may be a good idea to keep a list for yourself and see if there is some sort of pattern.

If you have come this far with your interest in working with spirit and learning about it, then stick to it.

Psychometry

Psychometry is the art of "reading" an object. We all have an energy/auric field around us which holds a "data base" if you like of everything to do with us which rubs off on to everything we touch. This object can then be "read" by a psychic who should be able to pick up information about the owner of the item, where it has been stored, the owner's life and many related pieces of information.

Police sometimes use psychometry on murder weapons to try and ascertain something about the murderer, or where the weapon had been stored or bought. This type of information has lead to catching the culprit on many occasions.

Sometimes when you go for a reading with a medium, you will be asked to hand them an item personal to you often a piece of jewellery. The medium will then be able to link in to these energies. They may then be able to go a step further and make an actual link to Spirit.

As a new developing medium, holding an item belonging to your recipient may help you get a better connection to spirit for that person.

I have seen many people try this exercise and instantly say "I haven't got anything". You need to give yourself time. Sometimes, if we are in a group setting, we are scared of what people will think of us or think that we are making ourselves look silly. Let go of those feelings. Every medium has to go through the same processes. Everyone who starts off with anything new has to start off at the beginning, always remember that. It is important to take on board that we all develop skills, no matter what they are, at different rates.

Don't push yourselves too hard, just literally go with the flow and what will be will be, and your own speed will be determined. Always remember to be patient with yourself, and understand that not all exercises work for everyone. We will have our own niches as far as this work is concerned, the same as anything else, we can't all be good at numbers or good at swimming.

I was once was asked, during a reading, to psychometrise a cash tin – I don't particularly like psychometry. I held the cash tin and I trusted that the information I would get would be correct. Not only did I ascertain from its energies that money had been stolen from the tin, but also the amount of money, where the tin had been hidden (more than one place) and the initials of the two people that were suspected of stealing the money.

It is common courtesy to ask permission before doing any of these exercises.

Exercise No 16

Ask a friend if you can hold an item which belongs to them, perhaps a coin or piece jewellery. How does this make you "feel"? Depending upon how developed your psychic skills are, you should be able to sense something. Initially you may just get a sense of hot or cold. That's fine.

Now use your mind's eye/ third eye to show you images. Put the object in your hand and allow your mind to wander – like day dreaming. Just see what "pops" in to your mind. You may get pictures or feelings or words, but just allow your mind to be free and allow these thoughts to come in to your head. The trick with this is not to try too hard.

If it feels more comfortable for you write down the information. This might make it easier for you by lessening the possibility of you looking silly in front of someone else.

Remember it doesn't matter how silly the information appears to you, it could be so spot on and relevant to your recipient. So trust it all.

Exercise No 17

Working in a group setting get someone to sit in the centre of the circle. Psychically link in to their energies and do a reading this way.

You could ask to be given answers to questions such as:

What was this person doing today?
What was going on with them say when they were about 10 years old?
Are they married?
Do they have children?
Any major illnesses – what age?
What is their house like?
Have they had any work done around the house recently?
Is their house clean and tidy?
Do they like their housework?

Exercise No 18

Remote viewing – this is when a medium uses their mind to see events at a distance and was used in the Cold War by the military.

Again you need to get permission from the person you are working with.

Link in to the energies of the person and get a feel of their house.
Stand outside their front door. What does it look like, colour, can you see a number?
What does the garden look like?
Walk in through the front door. Is there a hallway?
Is it a house or a bungalow? How are the rooms set out?
Walk around and see if you can get a sense of colours, type of furniture etc
What is underneath your feet?
Look out of the windows and see what you can see
Is there a garden?

Exercise No 19

Telephone numbers

Write a telephone number down on a piece of paper. Preferably a number of someone who is still in the physical world and someone that is known to the person you are working with (your partner). Exchange papers with your partner.

Imagine that you are dialling that number in your head.

"Hear" it ring and wait for the phone to be picked up.

Who has picked it up, male or female?

Allow your mind to wander – daydreaming again - and then watch as you are shown your images.

Like the remote viewing ask yourself the same sort of questions and watch and see what happens.

Children
Is it an imaginary friend?

"The most interesting information comes from children, for they tell all they know and then stop"... Mark Twain

Children are amazing at understanding, believing, seeing and communicating with spirit. They have no fears and just accept. They are born intuitive. If they are encouraged to stimulate this faculty by using their imagination, they will never lose it. If parents encouraged a positive self image from a young age it can make all the difference to your child's latter health and happiness.

So many children, when they are very young have "imaginary friends", but are they? I think nowadays people are more aware of spirit being around. I used to hear parents telling their children, "don't be so stupid" or "it's just your imagination". I do think people are more accepting now, or I would like to think they are. One of my own sisters who had an imaginary friend called "mischievous" who used to go everywhere with her. We just used to laugh at her.

I have 3 of the most wonderful children, Neil, Gareth and Victoria who I am very proud of and they never stop ceasing to amaze me with their efforts in this life. They are all very spiritual and all have an awareness of spirit.

Neil and Victoria had their awareness from very early ages however Gareth didn't get his awareness until the age of twenty eight. At that time in his life he was having a few difficulties, new job, new country, homesick, unwell, lonely and I feel spirit were just letting him know in a reassuring sort of way that they were there for him too, looking out for him.

Gareth is a scientist and I feel his brain works more logically. He does not want to "believe" in all this and I'm sure thinks I am totally mad and still can't get his head round what his mum does for a living. When he was first at university he asked "how come you all see things (meaning Spirit) and I don't". I tried to explain to him that I thought his mind worked more logically.

My eldest son Neil was just 4 when he was "seeing" spirit. At the time I knew about spirit but was not working with it and I was far from where I am now with my beliefs. However I did not discount his claims because of my own childhood sightings. I remember speaking to my Mum about Neil's experiences, she told me that it was probably either his imagination, he was hallucinating or dreaming; OR that he was really seeing something. She said not to mention it to him and just see what happened, whether he said anything more about it to me. I overheard him mentioning it again to one of his friends one day so I decided to question him about it. He described a lady that "came from the light in his ceiling". His description fitted my Grandmother exactly. The same lady that I had been seeing from the age of eight and of course a relative he had never met.

I asked if he was frightened by this and he said "no she won't hurt me, she just holds my hand and talks to me". I think my children have been lucky in that I understood what was happening with them and accepted it and got them to accept that this was the norm. Part of their everyday living.

When my daughter Victoria was two years old she talked about the man who came to play with her and who played a recorder like hers. She then went on to describe my Grandfather who played a Clarinet, which to a two-year-old would I suppose resemble a recorder. She also had another family member who "let her make a mess and didn't shout about it", which she thought was funny. I was a lot further into my spiritual beliefs at this time so it was easier for me to understand what was happening and why. We often talked about her spirit visitors as on occasions she ended up with several spirit friends being with her. We had Lizzie and Boyfriend, (her names for them) whom she described in such detail. They used to come everywhere with us, to the supermarket, on holiday, everywhere. When we went in the car Lizzie would have to have a seatbelt on and a seat in the trolley at the supermarket.

Boyfriend, however was a naughty little boy and would sit on the dashboard of the car and refused to wear a seatbelt. I used to ask her about her "friends" quite often and she would actual tell me how they were dressed. She also described the way that Boyfriend had died. He had been told by his father not to go into the woods with his friends. He had been warned about a dangerous pool. Apparently he didn't listen, went near the pool of water and was drowned.

We also had a little girl that used to pop up in the bathroom. She always came out from behind the shower screen. I asked Victoria one day, where the girl came from, meaning who was she? She replied "I don't know from the plug hole I think". This little girl did frighten her a little because of the way that she jumped out at Victoria from behind the screen. We talked about this and I told her to tell her spirit friend not to do it. She did and it worked.

I used to ask her periodically whether her "friends" were with her and she would either say yes or no. If no I would ask where were they and she would reply "gone to visit their mums and dads I think". Many years later, I think she was about thirteen, and I asked her were her "friends" still around. She answered yes. So I said to her that she didn't mention them any more and I was so amused by her reaction. She said, "well, you know that they're there, and I know that they're there, so why do I have to mention it!" Kids eh?

As I have said several times in this book, I was eight years old when I was first consciously "aware" that there was something else around that grown-ups couldn't see. I was very shy as a little girl and didn't tell people about my sightings, but I didn't think it was unusual either, they were always there with me. Actually it's really great as it was my Grandmother on my dad's side that I have always seen and I know that she is still always there, working with me on a daily basis.

Children do not have any hang-ups or prejudices and they tell it as it is. I recently ran a workshop for nine to fifteen year-olds, it was amazing. The children just knew that they had spirit around them. They *knew* that they could talk to them. They *knew* that they would talk back to them. They just *knew* and *accepted*, like it was such a natural thing! They were NOT scared. I was delighted to see how unrestricted they were and how comfortable they were knowing that the "ghosts" "spirits" were with them all the time.

We really do need to go back to basics and do as the children do:- trust, know, believe, and NOT to be frightened.

I recently had an opportunity to spend time with two boys aged nine and seven. Their mother told me they talked about spirit people and animals all the time and asked if I would come and have a chat to them about it. When I arrived I was met by two very normal, very intelligent young men I asked them about what they see and how. They automatically took their focus off me and then looked into the space by the side of me (this is something I have learned to do as a medium in order to get a clearer picture of spirit) and they came up with all sorts of wonderful things. The spirit people who were in the room with us, the animals they saw and felt. They took great pride in showing me with their hands the outline of their dog which had passed to spirit. They also told me about what they saw in auras, how they saw it, including colours, and what they saw in mine!

It is a shame adults don't always have the ability to do this. We just try too hard, whereas children just do it!

Healing

"Having opened the door of hope I know my spirit will soar and untold wonders will be revealed" ... Betty Shine

You don't have to be psychic or a sensitive to be a healer. We are all born with the abilities to connect to spirit in either way. Many people are natural healers and don't realise it, which is a shame, think how much good we could all do if we realised that this God-given ability was there naturally and we could use it for so much good.

A healer has just as many abilities as the psychic/sensitive/medium but they are often heard to say "I am not psychic, I am a healer". Healing power is a psychic energy. The healer will ask spirit to work with them in the healing process and is then able to direct the healing energies to the recipient. Healers will often be able to pick up in their own body indications of where the pain or illness is with the recipient.

The healing part of what I do is so important to me also. When I first got involved at West Wickham Church I also started training to be a healer. I was taught that spiritual healing was a three way process. This means that the healing energies come from spirit beings who have passed on, through the healer's Spirit, and then to the Spirit of the person receiving the healing. It works!

From spirit, through spirit, to spirit.

Imagine the auric/energy field around you, and also around spirit. When you ask for spirit to work with you, be it for healing or mediumship, those two auric/energy fields overlap. You have the recipient, the person you are healing in front of you and you and your spirit healers energy is now overlapping with their energy field. This merging of the energies then allows the healing process to happen. This is explained again in the chapter on energy on page 65.

When you are in the healing mode try scanning your own body to feel the problem area of your recipient. The more you try this the easier it will become. Practice is always the key with everything we do and the same goes for healing.

It is important to remember that it is not for a healer to diagnose. Only a qualified medical person should do this.

I really enjoyed my healing classes, however when I was doing my healing I kept getting messages from spirit which, according to the training at the time, I was not supposed to be doing. The teaching then was that you were either a healer giving healing, or a medium giving messages. I realised that I had to be doing both so could not continue the healing programme within the church.

Healing within churches or other centres is very important and more and more people are looking for spiritual healing. It works.

Now I do mainly "absent healing". This is healing at a distance. Asking spirit to send healing to people anywhere in the world who are in need of help. Anyone can do it. You just have to know, trust and believe that you have spirit with you, and you just ask them to send healing, helping hands to whoever you know that is in need. You can also ask for help for yourself.

When I started on my spiritual journey I had such a thirst for knowledge and read so many books on the subject. Betty Shine books were like my Bible at the time. I just picked up the book and opened at a page and I was always guaranteed it would be relevant to me at the time. It was a healing. Betty Shine was an amazing medium and healer. Many of her books have her picture on the front cover and this to me was enough. Just looking at this beautiful lady's face made me feel so much better.

One day, on my way to work in London, I was reading one of her books and came to the point where she said about sending out healing to people around you. She said imagine you have a laser beam of light coming from you to the person you want to heal and know it works. So I thought I would give this a go.

On the train that day was a man who had obviously broken his leg. He was on crutches and heavily plastered. As we were getting off the train I decided to give this a go. Why not, the man was obviously in pain. So I sent my laser light of healing out to him and I could not believe what happened next, he fell over! I was so shocked. It was funny and I felt so bad. I make sure now that I am a little more gentle when doing this exercise.

You can practice this on people. If you are sitting with others around you try the laser light experiment. You will notice that people will turn around, almost like they feel someone looking at them, like someone has tapped them on the shoulder. I used to try this on buses and trains. It is quite interesting how often it works. Give it a try.

When my aunt and uncle were still alive in Australia I heard that my uncle had had a stroke. Automatically I started sending healing his way. A few years later I was lucky enough to spend my 40th birthday with them in Australia. At this time because of several strokes, he had become quite poorly and was unable to communicate well, except with close family.

One day on this trip I was sitting with my aunt and uncle in their home and my uncle started crying. He started muttering something which only my aunt could understand. She said that for quite a long time before I had visited them he kept telling her about this blue light he kept seeing, with stars and a face in it. He did not recognise the face.

My aunt and uncle had gone to Australia when I was 8 years old so he would not have recognised my adult face. What he had been trying to tell my aunt that day that it was my face he had been seeing amongst the stars and blue light. I then explained to them about absent healing and told them what I had been doing.

Sadly my uncle died not long after my visit. Shortly after his death my aunt telephoned me. She asked if I was still sending my blue lights. I told her that I was as I felt that she needed healing due to her loss. I was delighted when she told me that the blue lights were coming out of the cupboard where the urn with my uncle's ashes were kept.

My Aunt has since passed and I "see" both of them regularly and they continue to help me with my work for Spirit.

I have also found many fantastic web sites where you can put a name down for healing and these healing messages go right across the world, and what is wonderful is that I get messages from healers across the globe that are sending their healing thoughts to these people whose names I have put forward for healing.

It is my belief that sometimes we are not meant to heal the ailment but help with the transition to the spirit world. The body may be too sick to recover but we can help the spirit of that person come to terms with their situation. I have helped a number of people in this situation. They know they are not going to get well, but they are more accepting of what is going to happen to them and where they are going.

I had a great friend who came to see me for a reading when suffering with advanced Cancer. She knew that I could not cure her cancer but soon after the reading sent me a card with the message "I have spent over two years terrified of my cancer and of the voices in my head. One hour with you and everything fell into place. I feel safe, in control and alive. You have given me my life back and helped me escape from the saddest place in the universe. You have given my boys their mum back and my husband his wife. You will always have a special place in my heart. I can't thank you enough."

What I will say here is that it was not me at all, it was the wonderful mystical energies that are around us at all times.

My eldest son had a very dear friend who had cancer for many years and unfortunately she lost her battle a few years ago. He would visit her regularly and talk to her about death and what was to come. This helped her in many ways to come to terms with what was happening to her and in some ways made it easier for her. So he had helped/healed her without him even realising that was what he was doing.

My daughter from the age of seven always had girls from school coming to her with their problems. They were instinctively drawn to her. At the time she did not realise what she was doing, that by just talking to them she was healing. She used to come home from school and ask "why do they all come to me with their problems".

When she was very little, I had problems with my lungs, and she would automatically come and sit with me and put her arms round me with her hands on my upper back. The heat that used to emanate from her palms was amazing and it always made me feel so much better.

Healing can also be sent to animals. Try this on your pet next time they are unwell. Try it on your plants too. You hear about people who talk to their plants, well do this and touch them and watch them improve.

When holding teaching classes at my home I always have glasses of water for the students. If there was any water left over I used to throw it away. One day something told me to put this water on my plants. The spiritual energies in the room when we are working is very charged, and guess what, my plants look amazing. So the healing powers in the water have helped the plants too.

The acceptance of spiritual healing is growing and there are many centres across the world where you can go and not just in spiritual churches. Some of these are listed at the end of this book and many more can be found on the internet.

Astral Travel

"A phenomenon in which a person feels separated from his or her physical body and seems to be able to travel to, and perceive, distant locations on Earth."

I have had a few experiences of Astral travelling which still amaze me.

When my daughter was about fourteen, I woke up one night, after having been asleep for a while. I am not sure what actually woke me up, but there I was awake and there at the end of my bed was my daughter, Victoria. She was standing there in her pyjamas, smiling at me. I suddenly realised that I could hear her snoring in the next room. So she was asleep in her own room and yet there she was standing at the end of my bed smiling at me.

Another occasion, this time when she was about eighteen, Victoria was preparing to go out for the evening. She had told me that she would be staying out, so not to wait up for her. I locked up and went to bed. At about 1.30am I was woken up suddenly by her opening my bedroom door, and then talking to me. With me now sitting up in my bed she told me about her evening and when I questioned her about not staying out, she told me that she decided to get a cab home. After a few minutes she said good night and off she went to bed.

In the morning, I got up and was going about my business in the house, trying to be quiet in order not to wake her as she had come home so late. At 10.30am the front door opened and in she walked. I was so surprised to see her arrive and even more surprised when she told me about her night out which was exactly as I had heard her tell me at 1.30am.

Spirit Guides and Helpers

We all have spirit guides/helpers/guardian angels who are there to help protect us and help us with our spiritual progression.

Some people are really obsessed by the name of their guide, where they came from, their era, age, and many other details. I don't think it matters who the guide is, they are there to help with our progress and our acceptance of this will enhance how they work with us and how our work progresses.

We just need to know that they will work with us at all times and will give us the tools we need to make progress. They will never let us down. Our acceptance of this is important. They will guide us to the right people, the people they know we can help and to the people that can help us. They will also guide us as to what way we work with our psychic development. They know better than us, how best we can work for and with them.

They are there for the development of our psychic gift and in turn the helping of others. We have our own physical choices to make and our own spiritual path to follow, we have our own personal responsibility.

Psychic Self Defence

Evil spirits

In all the years I have been working with spirit, I have never come across an evil spirit. I simply never let anything other than good spirits draw close to me. They may be out there, but I have never encountered one.

I may have been scared in the past, but this was because I was just inexperienced and did not understand what was going on around me. I now know differently.

I have even done ghost investigations and still not encountered anything bad, even in places where really horrific things have happened. You will find that as you develop your ability to open yourself up to the spirit world you become more sensitive. Everything around you will seem much more intrusive, noise louder, bustle and crowds more distressing, this can be quite unsettling if you don't realise why this is happening.

Remember that we are surrounded by vibrating energy and as we learn we expand our energy in turn becoming more sensitive to these external forces around us.

As a psychic you can consciously or unconsciously become attached to some of these streams of energy. These invisible forces/energies are not evil or necessarily unfriendly but they can be draining. Think of allowing spirit connection as inviting someone into your house. You would not invite everybody and anybody into your home, you would be selective. Then when your friends leave, you shut the door behind them, therefore closing the door also to unwanted intruders. This is exactly what we have to do with the spirit world and the way you should continue to practice your psychic development. Leaving yourself open all the time can be draining; you can have unwanted "visitors" which could affect you in various ways.

Our guides and helpers will protect us when we are working, but it is up to us to make sure that we protect our physical selves in between.

I hear from students that they are still "open" even though they have closed themselves down. In the early stages, we need to be firmer with spirit, be precise in your instructions to them. Tell them when you are working and when you are not.

You will find, because of your enthusiasm, you are constantly talking about spirit and the mere thought of them can bring them back in. If this happens you will be open to all the energies around you stepping in and it can lower your normal vibrations. This in turn can affect your personality, your sleep patterns, your energy levels, and you may end up with exhaustion, depression, anxiety irritability, which may be totally out of character.

This is not good. So to practice "opening up" and "closing down" is vital. You must try to get this balance between when you are working and open to spirit and not.

Even psychic conversation, that is you talking to spirit for yourself for instance, you have just opened yourself back up! Remember to close down afterwards.

If you take care of your spiritual equipment, then your guides will be able to use you in the best possible way and improve the quality of your mediumship. If intrusions keep happening it means that you are doing something wrong. This is you doing it wrong not spirit. Remember personal responsibility always. Go back retrace your actions, and reaffirm your intentions. Be very determined and make sure that you are actually closed down. You may need to tell them a few times to start with, but eventually they and you will get the message. Thought alone can open you up, so do be aware.

When you are beginning your work with spirit, they will often work with you at night, this may result in you not sleeping properly. Before you go to sleep ask spirit to let you wake up rested, no matter what work they are doing with you. I guarantee this will make a difference.

During my sleep, spirit used to take me to the Halls of Knowledge, which is a place in the spirit realms where they can teach us the tools we need to be working with them.

I read a book by Ivy Northage which explains 'Evil Spirits' so much better that I could. She says "I am often asked if psychic activity invites evil spirits. Accepting a reasonable and sensible approach to all such phenomena, the answer is a positive *no*. Like attracts like, and someone sincerely desirous of developing their gifts for the good of humanity cannot be in touch with evil."

Remember that you are always in control. If you want spirit there they will be, if you don't they won't be. As simple as that, don't forget it. If you are connecting to the spirit world with the right intention you will have only

good spirits with you.

Death
What is it that we fear?

During our physical lifetime our "body" is the vehicle we use to exist. When death comes in the physical world, this vehicle has no further use and ceases to be. Our spirit does NOT die. Why should it? The spirit or soul or essence of us continues to exist but in a different dimension. Around us and with us all the time.

We are all the same, we all have the same fears about death. It is not until it is proved to us that death is not the end that we can lose this fear. This is what a good medium does for people who have suffered loss. They prove that the physical body may have passed but the spirit has not. How else then can they, the medium, give such information about a person they have never met and know nothing about. Who is telling them this? How do they know?

The good medium is able to give closure and comfort to those who have lost a loved one by giving information that will categorically prove that they are in communication.

People are afraid of death, of talking about it, of talking to someone who is grieving. How do I approach them? What do I say? Do I speak to them about? Do I change the subject and not mention? Will they cry if I mention it? If they do how will I deal with that? Will I get emotional? Is it right to get emotional in front of them?

When someone dies, it does not mean that they didn't exist. And 99% of the time the person who is grieving does want to talk about them and their lives, what they meant to them, the funny stories, etc... The emotion has to come out, it has to be shown. Bottling this up just causes pain. The majority of the time, the people who have suffered loss are proud of this person and want to share this as much as they can. So many times one hears of people who have lost someone dear to them and friends will do all of the above, change the subject, not phone them, not contact them. This is so very hurtful and upsetting to the person grieving.

Why is this? Some countries/nations deal with death differently and it is not a problem sharing in the grief. But I find in the UK especially people just don't know how to approach the subject or how to deal with it. We need to learn and to realise that by sharing and talking about such things, it will help the grieving people and ourselves. We need to learn to celebrate a person's life. It is their life we need to share in, celebrate, talk about, laugh about, cry about. All the silly little things, the bad things, the naughty things, the good things. It is not until someone dies that we talk about their lives; there were so many things about that person of which you were unaware. Even members your own family.

My Grandfather died at the age of eighty seven and at his funeral the vicar talked about his days as a prisoner of war. He was captured and escaped so many times. On his final escape along with a Canadian Soldier he mapped all the munitions dumps on a perilous journey up through Italy. When they arrived in allied territory they handed over these maps. As a result of this, these munitions dumps were destroyed by bombers and so many thousands of lives were saved. I am so proud, before his funeral I never knew.

I met a wonderful family who lost their seventeen-year-old son in a tragic accident. He was a typical seventeen-year-old in all the things he got up to. But as a result of people in their surrounding area coming forward and talking to the family, they found out some amazing tales about him, including that every Thursday evening he would go and get the old lady down the road her fish and chip supper. His Mum and Dad didn't know that. How wonderful that as a result of talking to them about their son this little unknown fact was shared with them.

One family told me of their Daughter/Sister who had passed recently. The Sister said how upsetting it was that her friends had stopped calling her. She said that they obviously didn't know how to handle the situation, but she felt abandoned by those she had felt she could trust. People die, but they still exist, it may not be physically but they will always be in our hearts, no matter what. We should remember that and not be afraid to talk, to ask, to speak about them. Do not be afraid to ask a grieving person how they are coping, and to learn to deal with their responses.

Talking about things is good. It is said "a problem shared is a problem halved". This sharing with the grieving is helping both them and you to come to terms with and accept the life of that person who did exist and still does.

The next time you have an opportunity to talk to someone who has recently lost someone dear to them, talk to them. Remember to be sensitive to their emotions but give them the opportunity of talking about how they feel. Be strong yourself. Send them healing energies – and yourself too if you are finding it difficult. Do it, remember the people we lose are real, they were here and are still here. Like a chapter to a book, it closes, but its still always there to be opened and read again.

When someone is dying why don't we talk to them about death and what to expect? Tell them that this won't be the end. We will be together again. They will be able to stay in touch with us when they go to spirit. This can be so comforting for both the person who is dying and the person(s) who are losing them. Why not make some plan/pact as to how you will show that you are still there.

My wonderful friend Mary Edwards did this with her son. Nobody knew except the both of them what their pact was. On the day of her funeral, at a packed crematorium, we were all singing "We'll meet again" and celebrating her life. To our amazement a bouncing ball of golden light was

dancing in time with the music, in and out of the congregation, and appearing to bounce off the song sheets and up and down the walls. This was not a reflection, there was no explanation for the light. After the service her son confirmed that this was what they had agreed would be the sign, the way in which she would let him know that she was still there with the family.

Measure of Success

There are many more places to learn mediumship skills.

Recommendation again is a must. Try taster weekends which are always great fun and will give you an idea of what you possibly want to do within mediumship.

Remember that your daily experiences of life will help to expand you as a person and you as a spiritual person and your spirit. As you grow in your spiritual work, so will you shine brighter. This will be seen by the physical and the spirit world.

It is important to recognise when you have outgrown your circle. If you feel unhappy or uncomfortable within your group, then it's time to move on. Don't be frightened to do so. People will understand. If they don't that's their problem not yours. As physical beings we are always worried that we are going to "upset" someone by saying we need to move on. The only one you are upsetting is yourself and spirit. They don't want you to be unhappy doing this work.

We should also recognise that we will not always work well with everyone. If a person is introduced to your group and you feel uncomfortable, you should speak up. If you can't do this, then it is time to move on. You are in a circle to improve your own abilities. Don't let others hinder or stop your progress.

The more learning environments you can experience the better. You need to be stretching your abilities at all times, no matter how far you have gone.

Your success is not measured by other people's opinion of you or your mediumship. Be honest with yourself. If you make a mistake, learn from it. Sometimes working with spirit can be a very difficult thing. We get up, we do our work, whether in a church, a private sitting or a theatre. Then afterwards we look back over what we have done and question, did I do that right? Should I have said that? Why did I....? If only ....?

Please don't do this, it is totally self-destructive. Just know that on that day with that particular work, you did exactly what was required of you by spirit. Don't "beat yourself up".

Learn as you go, take things on board, move forward and know that you are taking another step forward in the development of your successful mediumship. At the end of the day "the proof of the pudding is in the eating". If your recipient is happy with your reading, you have done what you were meant to do!

Remember

If you get it wrong when you're learning, you are entitled to do this.

Books sometimes make things look easy, but it certainly is not easy and it can take time.

I have had many years of ups and downs and many mistakes, but many great teachers, both physical and spiritual have helped to get me here.

Always be patient, the basics of any subject are so important to master otherwise you will not succeed, and progress will be slow.

Your helpers may be new to this and it takes time for them to adjust as well as you.

Some people will develop quicker than others. This is not a reflection on you, or your teacher, or spirit, we are just all different.

There is also no "right" way of doing this. We will all work differently and this is important.

Teaching is always guided learning. Someone else's way of doing something is not necessarily the right way for you. So take the guidance but remember to try and be individual not a clone.

ALWAYS be respectful and polite. Never be offensive or humiliating at any time. You are dealing with people's emotions when working between spirit and your sitter and you have to be careful what you say and how you say it. This applies equally in public or in private.

Enjoy working with spirit. If you don't, then stop doing it. Simple as that. This should be a partnership with the spirit world that is fun and encouraging. Be rewarded by the knowledge that you are helping people every day by comforting and linking them to their loved ones.

Try not to ask questions of your sitter either as this will look like you are "fishing for information".

NEVER give bad information. I have heard this all too often, where a medium has given information that was very distressing to the recipient. We do not have the "right" to do this.

We can't make decisions for people. It is up to each individual to make their own choices. Spirit are there to guide and help us, not to tell us what to do. We have our earthly life with our earthly choices. People will come for readings wanting to know if they are going to meet someone? Should they leave their husband, a whole range of direct questions. Remember you are not a fortune teller.

You will be "given" your information in different ways. This could come in the form of pictures, thoughts, feelings and you must learn to recognise these various methods. Trust that they are coming from spirit and NOT from you or your mind.

If you are looking for a medium, always go on recommendations. Either from a friend or through a body such as the Spiritualist National Union (SNU) who hold a list of recognised, qualified mediums.

If you have had any problems with depression, or your mental health, don't embark on spiritual development before speaking to someone such as a recommended medium, or member of one of the spiritualist bodies.

Always be true to yourself, and spirit. Never make things fit and never make things up.

If you are "working" and you get nothing, be honest and say that.

Charging for a reading. I was told once by a wonderful teacher, Janet

Parker that if you provide a good service you should be remunerated. If you call out a plumber, or a carpenter you pay him. Don't be greedy, but spirit know that you have to pay your bills.

You never stop learning. I learn daily from the sittings and teaching that I do, and still do training courses where I can. Get as much training and knowledge from books as you can.

Go into a sitting or mediumship demonstration with an open mind. If you go with preconceived ideas you will block the energies and not get a good clear reading or a connection to the person you want to hear from.

Conclusion

"Do not believe in anything simply because you have heard it. Do not believe in anything simply because it is spoken and rumoured by many. Do not believe in anything simply because it is found written in your religious books. Do not believe in anything merely on the authority of your teachers and elders. Do not believe in traditions because they have been handed down for many generations. But after observation and analysis, when you find that anything agrees with reason and is conducive to the good and benefit of one and all, then accept it and live up to it."

Buddha

There are a lot of people out there who will take your money – charlatans – those who will pray on the vulnerable - be careful.

I get very upset when I hear of unscrupulous mediums, and they are out there. They will tell people what they think they should be hearing or what they think they want to hear. Finding a good medium should be done through recommendation or through any of the bodies listed at the end of this book.

So why do people go to a medium?

Most people will go to a medium because they have lost a close friend or relative and want confirmation that they are, for instance, out of pain, or forgive them, or are happy on the other side or that they are just there. Other people will go to a medium as they want to know what is going to happen to them. They seek guidance for the future.

Go with your instincts on choosing a medium. You will find that you are drawn to someone who has empathy with you, similar experiences, similar lives, or just someone you feel comfortable with.

For any of you new developing mediums out there, I would also like to point out that, for some reason, in this work there can be a lot of jealousy. If you do your work and learning with the right intent, spirit will always be there for you and with you.

I have had many experiences of this jealousy over the years, where I was told I was not old enough, not experienced enough, I don't sit in a development circle any more, why do I think I can get up and do a theatre, who do I think I am!!!!

Well I will tell you from me that I KNOW as long as I am working for spirit with the right intention and I do not harm anyone along the way, and only aim to help and heal, spirit will always be there for me and I KNOW this as a fact.

I have recently made a pact with spirit, they got me doing this work, I know what I am supposed to be doing and why I am doing it and so do they.

So here I am and here I will stay. I am in for the long haul!

Although my journey so far had been long, I feel that this is still the beginning of my amazing journey, which is still in its infancy. There is so much more to come. I keep telling my friends I will be 92 when I die and I have so much to do between now and then.

"Let us endeavour to live so that when we come to die even the undertaker will be sorry"...Mark Twain

Mediumship Teaching

Courses

Spiritualist Association of Great Britain
33 Belgrave Square, London SW7 2EB
Tel: 0207 235 3351

The College of Psychic Studies,
16 Queensberry Place,
London SW7 2EB
Tel: 0207 589 3292

The Arthur Findley College of Psychic Studies,
Stanstead Hall,
Stanstead CM24 8UD
ENGLAND

Healing

Harry Edwards Sanctuary
National Federation of Spiritual Healers
Old Manor Farm Studio,
Church Street,
Sunbury on Thames, TW16 6RG
Tel: 01932 783164

"Yesterday is History, Tomorrow a Mystery, Today is a Gift, Thats why it's called the Present" … unknown

Further Reading

Mediumship Made Simple, Ivy Northage, The Psychic Press 1986

Betty Shine, Mind Series, Corgi 1990

Psychic Development, William W Hewitt, Llewellyn Publications 2008

Enclyclopaedia of Mystical & Paranormal Experience,
Harpers, Castle Books 1991

The University of Spiritualism, Harry Boddington, Psychic Press